3-910944

720
SMI

35.00

Smith, G. E. Kidder
    Looking at
architecture

720
SMI

910944

35.00

Smith, G. E. Kidder
    Looking at
architecture

THE BRUMBACK LIBRARY
OF VAN WERT COUNTY
VAN WERT, OHIO

LOOKING AT ARCHITECTURE

LOOKING AT ARCHITECTURE

Text and Photographs by

G. E. KIDDER SMITH

Fellow, The American Institute of Architects

Harry N. Abrams, Inc., Publishers, New York

CONTENTS

FOR

A. K. S. + F. H. S.

WITH LOVE

GC os

Editor: Margaret Donovan
Designer: Bob McKee

Frontispiece: Jantar Mantar, Jaipur, India, see page 98.
The quotation from Ada Louise Huxtable on page 152 is copyrighted
by *The New York Times* Company. Reprinted by permission
Library of Congress Cataloging-in-Publication Data
Smith, G. E. Kidder (George Everard Kidder), 1913—
Looking at architecture / text and photographs by G. E. Kidder Smith
p.   cm. Includes bibliographical references. ISBN 0–8109–3556–2
1. Architecture—Themes, motives.   I. Title.
NA200.S57 1990   90–30728
720—dc20   CIP

INTRODUCTION

AS AN ARCHITECT, author, and sometime photographer, I have been fortunate—via a series of foundation grants—to "experience" many of the world's great buildings. This book represents a distillation of fifty years of probing and documenting a cross-section of encounters, from each of which I have come away enriched. The earliest photograph dates from 1937, the most recent ones were taken in the autumn of 1989.

My expeditions stemmed from a curious obsession: a concern for architecture. Its repute, though not seriously ill, is ailing. In perhaps quixotic fashion, I would like to help open more eyes to the provocative rewards of well-turned buildings in space. Though most of us are throughout the day surrounded by what passes for architecture, little of what we see is distinguished, while even fewer of the buildings' occupants care. It is time to look critically about, to make an understanding of architecture more a part of our lives and our culture: the great buildings will be more exciting, while we will be better equipped to handle the less great.

It should be understood that the following assessments and remarks are those of an inquisitive architect and critic and only an amateur historian. (I believe that the names and dates given are correct, but standard sources sometimes differ; an approximate chronological order has been followed in the layout.) The aim of this book is to perk interest in architecture via notable buildings from a broad range of cultures, not to trace their historical development. A number of brilliant architectural histories are now available: they can give both pleasure and information.

A word about the photographs: almost all of them were taken on the run, so to speak, as they were shot while traveling. Whereas there were times when I could come back later for better light, they were few. I generally spent no more than ten to fifteen minutes on a picture, whether I was outside or inside. Incidentally, as regards interiors, I know nothing about artificial lights and do not have any. I find that most large-scale interiors, such as churches, generally don't need them.

My favorite camera—used for all the earlier photographs in this book—was a 1938 Zeiss Juwel, a marvelous, compact machine that fitted into my attaché case even with extra lenses. It could do anything asked of it. After 9 × 12-cm filmpacks were no longer made, I bought, and still use today, a 1962 Swiss Sinar Expert view camera using 4 × 5-in. filmpacks. It is totally flexible—far more than I need! For nontripod infighting I rely on my 1961 Rolleiflex: it is simple to operate and trouble-free. For 35-mm Kodachrome I have a manual Nikon, nothing automatic. I generally put it on a tripod, often with a perspective-control lens.

As for picture-taking technique, I tend to solve many problems by squinting as I search for an elusive composition. This causes some passersby to wag their heads, but lets me concentrate on essentials. More important, I seek a picture *in* the subject, not *of* it. If one seeks a good composition, the building generally will take care of itself. Since almost all of the following photographs were taken on the run, as mentioned, film developing was done—and occasionally done in—by local photo labs. However I made the enlargements used for this book and printed them mostly on number 1 and number 2 grades of paper.

The following architectural panorama seeks to be an introduction to the stimulating delights of great buildings. Some of them, even in photographs, might impress us forthwith, others are more subtle. Architecture is the slate of mankind: on the palimpsests of the centuries—from which we are still learning—we are designing our future. With increased knowledge and concern, a better man-made world can evolve. It is hoped that this book will stimulate thoughts and action towards that world.

G. E. Kidder Smith, FAIA
New York, 1990

THE PYRAMIDS OF GIZA

CAIRO, FOURTH DYNASTY (2680–2560 B.C.)

THE PYRAMIDS SEEN today south of Cairo are but a sad memento of what they were some 4,600 years ago, when their polished limestone flanks played games with the sun. Then they dazzled with mathematical perfection as they "stormed the heavens" (Sigfried Giedion). Alas, their precisely cut sheathing slabs were too tempting to later builders, and the pyramids were long used as quarries. (There are more than seventy pyramids throughout Egypt.)

The pyramids at Giza—descendants of primitive "stepped" prototypes built in superimposed layers—are gigantic prisms unique in world architecture, mathematics at an ultimate scale. It is quite possible that Cheops's Great Pyramid (c. 2680 B.C.; *opposite, center*) consumed more dressed stone blocks than any structure ever built, an estimated 2,300,000 of them, averaging 2.5 tons each. It is generally thought that the blocks were moved on log rollers and sledges and then ramped into place. (The wheels of chariots seen on Egyptian wall reliefs date from after the Hyksos invasions of about 1710 B.C.)

Cheops's pyramid, like the others, forms a precise square in plan: it is 756 feet on each side, with a height of 481 feet. Its orientation, determined by its builders without benefit of compass, varies only minutely off the cardinal points. Herodotus determined in 450 B.C. that the square of its height equals the area of each triangular face.

Concealed within the lower center of each of the Giza pyramids are the pharaoh's tomb and funerary chapel, reached by an ingenious passage designed to foil grave robbers. In Cheops's pyramid, the entrance is 55 feet above ground and was once hidden under a carapace of limestone. Despite such precautions, the tombs—initially filled with a panoply of riches to ensure comfort for the deceased in the next life—did not survive unransacked for long.

Though what we find today is without its original grandeur, the pyramids still rank among the most impressive—and oldest—monuments created by man.

STONEHENGE

SALISBURY PLAIN, ENGLAND, C. 3100, 2100–1500 B.C.

EERILY LONELY ON A Wiltshire hillock, its megalithic fingers engaged in a pastoral dance around an inner altar, Stonehenge has fascinated mankind for four thousand years. Why—and how—it was built have puzzled generations. Certainly the sun at summer solstice was central to its layout, but it seems unlikely that the exact angles of moon cycles and eclipses were of importance to presumably unlettered farmers. Recent computer analyses of the disposition of the stones suggest a site-plan precision transcending agricultural needs. Was a deity involved? Were the mathematics of Stonehenge designed to be seen from above?

Though dates are disputed, recent data indicate that the earliest phase of Stonehenge began about 3100 B.C. This stage consists of a still visible circular ditch within which is a circle, about 284 feet in diameter, lined with fifty-six pits called Aubrey Holes (named for John Aubrey, who in 1663 "tooke a review" of Stonehenge for Charles II). These earthworks gradually eroded, but about 2100 B.C. a vast remodeling of the abandoned area took place that not only utilized the great circle but erected at its center a double row of eighty bluestones, each roughly a yard high and weighing four tons. These were set in a semihorseshoe shape focused on the sunrise at the summer solstice. Almost unbelievably, the stones were brought from Wales, a distance of almost 250 miles. How they were excavated and shipped is not known.

About a hundred years later, the third and major development of Stonehenge took place when a ring of enormous sarsen (local sandstone) blocks encircled the then almost vestigial bluestones and created the Stonehenge we see today. These blocks, some of them 22 feet high and weighing perhaps 45 tons, form a precise circle around the core. Not only are the stones well dressed, the lintels that top them are curved to match the circle (as can be seen in the photograph) and they are secured horizontally by tongue-and-groove joints and vertically to the upright stones by mortise-and-tenons integral with the stone! Within this circle are five trilithons (two uprights supporting a lintel) forming a horseshoe shape, again strictly turned towards the June 21–22 sunrise.

The Egyptian pyramids were oriented within a tiny fraction to the cardinal points, yet they seemingly made no further demands on the heavens. Stonehenge, however, was virtually an ongoing observatory. Though assailed by nature and quarried by man—thus today visually sad—the megaliths of Wiltshire constitute a milestone in society's seeking an axis of the eternal.

QUEEN HATSHEPSUT'S OBELISK

KARNAK, EGYPT, C. 1450 B.C.

THE GERMAN-AMERICAN ARCHITECT Mies van der Rohe (1886–1969) wrote, echoing Flaubert, that "God is in the details"—an apothegm he followed in his own elegantly precise buildings. Though it is unlikely that Mies had Egyptian obelisks in mind, the adage was anticipated, long before, by the detailing of Queen Hatshepsut's obelisk (*opposite*).

Americans relish their own "obelisk" to General Washington (see page 130); many have seen the one that pulls together the spaces in front of Saint Peter's in Rome (in A.D. 37, it was brought to Italy by Caligula); and the fortunate have visited the mighty obelisks in Karnak. Yet few travelers to Karnak approach Hatshepsut's masterpiece (*right, center*) closely enough to examine the craftsmanship and design felicity that characterize its inscriptions. (Though a heraldic feature of most ancient Egyptian temples, not all obelisks carried such paeans to their builders.) The carving on this 97-foot-high polished red granite shaft is almost jewel-like in its precision. Note, too, the graphic sophistication of the vertical inscription—"Given Life Like Ra Forever"—and the small-scale bands of hieroglyphics below, which describe the raising of the obelisk.

The Temple of Karnak itself is largely in ruins, but its 3,450-year-old obelisk remains to remind us of the brilliance of ancient Egyptian culture.

HYPOSTYLE HALL, TEMPLE OF AMUN

KARNAK, EGYPT, BEGUN 1350 B.C.

IT IS DOUBTFUL IF any building yet designed has attained the dramatic power of the hypostyle hall of the Egyptian temple. Hypostyles—the Greek root means "resting on columns"—were man-made stone forests separating the temple's open court, where festivals and ceremonies took place, from the sanctuary, to which only kings and priests were admitted. (Egyptian temples did not provide for congregational worship.) The processional path through the hypostyle was a preparatory passage from this world to the next.

The hypostyle of the Temple of Amun, the most prodigious ever erected, was finished by Rameses II (d. 1225 B.C.) as an extension of an existing temple that had its origins a thousand years earlier and had experienced additions throughout its long life. This stone bastion of 134 columns delimits one side of the temple's Great Court and measures 338 feet wide by 170 feet deep. The columns defining the processional aisle are 69 feet high, the others 42 feet, the difference in height filled by a stone grille or clerestory. The entire hypostyle was originally roofed with slabs of stone: the effect of columns vanishing into darkness must have been spellbinding. We can bow to it today.

As seen in the photograph, the sandstone columns—with lotus bud capitals—are covered with hieroglyphics: they depict the deeds of the king, the names of the gods, and the history of the building.

Architecture has rarely produced such titanic theater.

THE TEMPLES OF PAESTUM

ITALY, 530–460 B.C.

IN A CURIOUSLY UNPREPOSSESSING landscape on the Gulf of Salerno, 50 miles south of Naples, three ancient, roofless Greek temples stand uniquely side by side in forlorn peace. The melancholy atmosphere was not always thus, for this once-walled outpost of Magna Graecia was for hundreds of years a flowering community. Founded about 600 B.C., Paestum, or Poseidonia as it was called until the Romans conquered it (273 B.C.), flourished under Augustus (63 B.C.–A.D. 14), then suffered from malaria as the river silted up, fell to the Saracens (A.D. 871), and was ransacked by Robert Guiscard (A.D. 1076). Paestum became uninhabited, indeed forgotten, for centuries until adventurous "antiquaries"—chief among them Johann Joachim Winckelmann, the great German archaeologist—"rediscovered" it in the 1750s.

Not only were the ruins then made widely known, but an enthusiastic appreciation of Greek art and architecture was also sparked. It should be remembered that, at this time, the Acropolis in Athens was covered with a miscellany of buildings, while the Parthenon itself was half hidden in a working mosque. The clear, unobstructed temples at Paestum thus came as a revelation. Because of Paestum, the Classic Revival was born with Greece, not Rome, ascendant.

The three Paestum temples are all in the Archaic Doric style of heavy columns with capitals that are squat, or as Goethe termed them, "oppressive." By the time the Parthenon was finished (438 B.C.), columns were elegantly slender, capitals had an alert, load-bearing profile, and refinement attended every detail. Moreover, they were carved from Parian marble; Paestum's now crudely exposed shellstone shafts, it is only fair to say, were originally covered with lime stucco. As in Greece proper, the temples at Paestum face easterly so that the rising sun will awaken the statue within.

The southernmost of the temples (*opposite, background*), the Basilica, was built about 530 B.C., with the Temple of Poseidon (*opposite, foreground*) dating from about 460 B.C. The third, farther north and not visible here, is the Temple of Ceres, from about 510 B.C. The Basilica is unusual in that it has nine columns across the ends and a row of columns down the middle of the interior: unfortunate on the exterior and inconvenient within for placing a cult statue. The newer and larger Temple of Poseidon is one of the best preserved of all Greek temples: even its double lineup of superimposed interior columns is still largely intact.

Paestum and its lonely landscape have an eerie, intriguing quality perhaps unequaled in the ancient world. More important, its revelation of Greek culture was of seminal influence in the Great Enlightenment of the eighteenth century.

THE PARTHENON

ATHENS, 447–438 B.C.

THE WORLDWIDE INFLUENCE of the Parthenon through two millennia is unprecedented. For many, it represents the canonization of architecture, the grail of a culture whose refinement in building has never been equaled.

When finished, the Parthenon was the perfection of a prototype (originally, of wooden members translated into stone) that had begun well over a century

earlier. It was designed as a windowless marble box resting on a three-step stylobate (stepped base; *opposite*) and surrounded by eight columns on the two ends and seventeen on the sides—the usual rule of twice the ends plus one. A door to the east, to catch the morning sun, and one at the west provided the only openings. Its details are legendary: the swelling profile (entasis) of its Doric columns, their closer placement at the corners (to compensate for open space beyond), the slight upward curvature of the stylobate (to counter visual sag), were only the most prominent optical refinements in this, the most meticulously studied building in history. Every line, every relationship, was impeccable—and still is.

It should be remembered, however, that our present enthrallment is based on conditions that did not obtain when Ictinus and Callicrates handed over the keys of the completed building in 438 B.C. The Parthenon then was only half visible from the Propylaea (the entry onto the Acropolis), since a line of service buildings blocked the view of the lower part. Moreover, the Acropolis itself was not of its present windswept purity, but accommodated a prominent statue of Athena, a series of terrace walls, and various ancillary structures.

Today in semiruins (since a wartime explosion in 1687), the Parthenon offers unequaled architectural-spatial experiences as it crowns the Acropolis. Through its now roofless skeleton, arrows of sunshine sweep across broken columns, while walls jump with shadows, the whole vibrating under the Attic sun. Walking within it, the observer is an explorer, not just an onlooker, for every movement generates fresh and mercurial images.

It can be argued, thus, that this noble structure delivers greater architectural impact with today's broken bones than it would if totally intact. (For reference, note the similar and nearby Theseion described on page 22: though nearly intact, it is lifeless.) An eager mood stirs as one approaches the Parthenon today: at which altar does one worship—as is or as was?

THE ERECHTHEION AND PROPYLAEA

ATHENS, 421–409 B.C.

HIGH AMONG THE rewards of the Acropolis are its strolling pleasures, especially the unexpected building and space interactions. Excursions begin when one steps from the fold of the Propylaea: excitement does not falter until one leaves. Among the most breathtaking vistas is the sudden encounter of the Propylaea from the Erechtheion (*opposite*).

The Erechtheion itself (*right*) is a curious structure, its plan reputedly compromised by sacred spots on the Acropolis, Athena's olive tree, and various program changes. In addition, its architect had to deal with a sharp grade drop-off. The result is a shrine with two stories on the north side and one on the south—producing four totally different facades. The result, though puzzling, deals admirably with its problems. Moreover, it is a refreshingly unsymmetric Classic building.

The airily scaled north porch with its six Ionic columns frames the view shown of the Propylaea plus a panorama of Athens. The south side of the Erechtheion, which faces the Parthenon, is rightly famous for its porch with six maidens—the caryatids—supporting the entablature (horizontal topping). The west end faces the Propylaea.

Used as a Byzantine church—which helped to preserve it—then, surprisingly enough, as the villa of an official, the Erechtheion suffered through the centuries. Even today some details are uncertain, but the twentieth-century restorations are excellent—as is its compact asymmetry.

THE THESEION

ATHENS, 449 B.C.

THE THESEION, OR Hephaisteion as it is also called, stands near the north flank of the Acropolis, thus just below the Parthenon, which was begun two years later. Its encircling columns—six across the ends, thirteen on the sides—are, surprisingly, still as built, as is the simple Doric entablature. The cella (sanctuary) wall is intact, but without its roof, and optical refinements abound. (The temple's good condition is due to the fact that it was converted into a church in the sixth century.) From a few viewpoints, such as in the photograph opposite, the Theseion can generate electricity with a slash of sun and shadow, but from most angles it is lifeless.

Is its perfection its weakness?

THE HORSES OF SAINT MARK'S

VENICE, 4TH–3RD CENTURY B.C.

THE FOUR MAJESTIC gilt-bronze horses that now prance over the main entrance to Saint Mark's Cathedral were sculpted in Greece, probably in the fourth or third century B.C. (Though this date is not universally subscribed to, when one considers that Phidias, the greatest sculptor of ancient Greece, lived from about 500 to about 432 B.C., such chronology seems acceptable.) The horses were taken to Rome, where they adorned Nero's triumphal arch and then that of Trajan, until Constantine sent them to the capital of his Byzantine Empire. In 1204 they were brought back to Italy as spoils of war and installed on Venice's Saint Mark's. Napoleon took them to Paris in 1798 as another spoil, but they were returned to Venice in 1815.

In spite of these peregrinations, they have come down to us intact (although, because of air pollution, they will probably have to be replaced eventually by copies). Placed on the upper terrace of the church, the horses, five feet tall, not only command the entry to the cathedral but the famous square in front as well. Sculpture also adorns Sansovino's library of 1540 (see the distant figures *opposite, lower right*).

The horses are quite possibly the finest example of large-scale animal sculpture ever made, and the skill in their casting lags not far behind their artistry.

THE FORUM

ROME, 1ST CENTURY B.C. – 4TH CENTURY A.D.

THE ROMAN FORUM was not simply the core of an ancient city; for many it was the center of the universe. From the birth of the empire under Augustus in 31 B.C., and for nearly five hundred years thereafter, Rome ruled—with lacunae—most of what we call the civilized world. From Scotland to the Sahara (see Timgad, page 30), and from Gibraltar to the Euphrates, the Roman Empire was in control. Moreover, Rome was the handmaiden of our alphabet, a bellwether of urban organization and its legal institutions, and the creator of startling new horizons in architecture.

The epicenter of this vast empire, Rome itself, strangely puzzles. The city was (and is) a jumble of forums, baths, circuses, temples, and basilicas of presumptuous self-importance, with little of the coordination one might expect from its efficient builders. Most of these structures are long gone, picked apart for their stones or buried under a thousand years of debris. However, in the Roman Forum we have inherited tantalizing hints of the city's confused—but fantastic—past.

Here, in the valley of the famous seven hills, layers of detritus gradually covered (and protected) much of the Capitoline Temple (*opposite, left*), the stalwart facade of the Temple of Saturn (*right*), the three columns of the Temple of Castor and Pollux (*midground*), the Arch of Titus (half-hidden beyond), and the Upper Forum (amidst the trees, *right*). Today, wrapped by shards of history, one can explore these weathered stones and be haunted by ancient Rome's magnificence.

THE STADIUM OF
DOMITIAN

ROME, A.D. 92

DOMITIAN (A.D. 51–96), a son of the Emperor Vespasian (builder of the Colosseum), was a strict law-and-order emperor. He was known for his personal building plans, the most ambitious of which was this palace complex atop the hill overlooking the Roman Forum. With splendid views of the Forum to the north and the Circus Maximus to the south, and convenient to all the city, its site was ideal.

Although little remains of Domitian's palace today, the evocative ruins of its combined hippodrome and garden (*opposite*) carry a romantic, Pines-of-Rome nostalgia. The emperor, alas, became so despotic that his wife had him murdered.

CITY OF TIMGAD

ALGERIA, FOUNDED A.D. 100

TIMGAD, CALLED THAMUGADI by the Berbers who lived—as they still do—in the surrounding Aurès Mountains, was founded in A.D. 100 by Emperor Trajan as the southernmost outpost of the Roman Empire. Located on important crossroads about 100 miles south of the Mediterranean, the city was established in large measure as a "retirement village" for veterans and as a general cultural force for the area. Set in a rich upland plain 3,300 feet high, it eventually developed into a thriving city of 12,000 to 15,000 people, who in the fourth century adopted Christianity. In the seventh century, it had to be abandoned because of attacks from neighboring tribes.

The walled but unfortified city was laid out in the usual rigid Roman grid pattern. The extensive forum occupies the lower center, with the 3,500-seat open-air theater adjacent, while four major baths, a library, and the Capitoline Temple (*opposite*) constitute the other key buildings. Substantial houses and shops filled most of the blocks inside the walled core; the extensive but casually laid-out "suburbs" outside accommodated the rest of the population.

The Arch of Trajan (*right*) commands the west entry to the city's colonnaded main street, the Decumanus Maximus. (Note the wagon-wheel ruts in the limestone pavement.) The arch, partially restored in 1900, is 40 feet high. Carefully placed on a rise for added importance, it was never fully buried under the desert sand or the hillside mud, as was most of the city. Its three passages, the side two for pedestrians, could be closed by portcullises.

Of the Capitoline Temple, only restored Corinthian columns remain, but these forlorn shafts, 44 feet high, serve as fitting memorials to this city, for some 1,200

years largely hidden under the Sahara. Beginning in 1880, the French commenced clearing and excavating the ruins, a lengthy but rewarding process.

Though little visited, Timgad is a textbook city of the Roman Empire: may its ruins long be preserved.

THE BATHS OF CARACALLA

ROME, A.D. 212–216

THE EGYPTIANS CONSTRUCTED the most prodigious monuments in the history of architecture, as reference to their pyramids and temples will confirm. The Greeks took the art of building to such exquisite refinement, as epitomized by the Parthenon, that 2,400 years later we are still impressed. The Romans, in turn, threw vaults over previously unequaled spaces—and asked the people in. Roman architecture, although bowing to the needs of gods and emperors, thus created the first major public buildings of consequence. Some of them are yet to be surpassed.

The early lack of a good mortar was in part responsible for the fact that the vault had rarely been used before. When the Romans discovered the structural possibilities of volcanic pozzuolana and lime cement, they opened up radical new construction opportunities via vaults and domes. The great interior was made possible.

The infamous Caracalla (A.D. 188–217) was the emperor who extended Roman citizenship to all freemen in the empire—largely, it is held, to raise taxes for such projects as his wildly popular bath. In the many years of its greatness, the complex must have been staggering both in size and opulence: it originally accommodated some 1,600 bathers as well as other activities such as sports and theatricals. The underground vaulted facilities for servicing the *calidarium* (hot baths) and *tepidarium* (lukewarm baths) were incredibly complex. In semiruins today, the bath remains impressive, especially on summer evenings, when it is used for staging opera.

Its architectural impact stems from the embracing, three-dimensional out-reach of its spaces—so different from the "lateral" spaces in Egypt and Greece—and from the visitor's pleasure in being a sheltered "participant" in a building, not just an observer. The great exedra (half-round bay with partial roof), seen here, establishes with the arches in the background a continuity of geometry which pulls horizontally at the same time that the ruined vaulting snatches us upward. Stupendous.

THE TEMPLE OF BACCHUS

BAALBEK, LEBANON, MID-2ND CENTURY A.D.

BAALBEK—ITS BAAL (possessor) suggesting Old Testament lineage—became a major outpost of the Roman Empire under Augustus (31 B.C.–A.D. 14). Earlier the Greeks had called it Heliopolis, city of the sun (in addition to their city of the same name in Lower Egypt). Well favored by nature and in a fair position to control passage between the Lebanon and Anti-Liban mountains, Baalbek flourished as a Roman colony. It is possible that even caravans from the Silk Road passed by. In the seventh century decline began when Arab factions fought over the city, then Mongols sacked it, while later earthquakes, primarily that of 1759, leveled it. Notwithstanding these vicissitudes, what had once constituted a magnificent temple complex is still a mighty ruin. Gigantic masonry characterized its construction, with possibly the largest dressed stones moved by man: one partially excavated stone measures 72 feet long by 16 feet square.

The Temple of Bacchus, which many historians consider the best-preserved Roman temple of its size, is part of Baalbek's immense semiruins. Its peristyle of forty-two unfluted Corinthian columns (nineteen still standing) embraces sturdily preserved exterior walls. The approach to the cella or worship room (*opposite*) proclaims grandeur with its powerful scale. Note the tilted column (*left*), still held together by its original iron cramps, the perilous keystone over the portal (*upper right;* now stabilized), and the enormous fallen capital (*lower right*). The inner side walls of the nave are divided into bays by projected Corinthian half-columns to produce a series of superimposed niches, round-headed below, angled (pedimented) above, the latter originally with statues. The temple was roofed with cedar trusses.

The temple, however, is but a single aspect of the vast complex. Baalbek is unequaled for boldness of concept and skill in utilizing Herculean masonry.

HAGIA SOPHIA

ISTANBUL, A.D. 537

A DOME IS A structurally useful roof that in simple form requires little expertise to construct. Diminishing built-up circles of blocks of ice or layers of stone suffice for a domed room in arctic or temperate regions, while plaited reeds can produce one for hotter climates. Rome's Pantheon (A.D. 124)—the city's best-preserved Classic building—is topped by the finest dome of ancient times. With an unprecedented diameter of 142 feet, an oculus (circular opening) at its top,

and an inner height equal to its lateral diameter, the concrete dome of the Pantheon helps to form a glorious interior. However, it is a static space that transfixes the beholder, rooting him or her to one spot.

Some four hundred years later, Anthemius of Tralles and his nephew Isidorus of Miletus, both citizens of ancient Asia Minor, went to work for the Emperor Justinian in Constantinople. These architects, each an outstanding mathematician, took the dome and flung it into orbit, creating an inner space whirling to infinity. In the process, they produced one of the most audacious buildings in the history of architecture—Hagia Sophia (Greek for "Divine Wisdom"). On opening the doors on Christmas night A.D. 537 to dedicate this masterpiece, Justinian—in a bit of imperial one-upmanship—reputedly bypassed his architects and proclaimed, "I have surpassed even thee, oh, Solomon!"

Hagia Sophia not only flings the dome heavenward, it conspires with two hemicycles (half-domes) to roil the space laterally and to force the observer to move about. Giant pendentives (triangular sections of vaulting effecting the transition from a square base to a circular dome) lend arched support and scale to the dome itself. The shallow terra-cotta dome, 107 feet in diameter, is ringed with forty low, arched windows that make it seemingly float in space. (The first dome was too shallow and partially collapsed; it was replaced in 562 by the steeper, ribbed dome we see today.) Procopius, a contemporary Byzantine historian, wrote in his book *On Buildings* that the dome looked "as if suspended by a chain from heaven."

The interaction of dome, hemicycles, and pendentives creates an interior little short of a whirling tempest. Its impact rewards, even though the mosaics that once enriched this celestial geometry are now largely gone.

KAILASA TEMPLE

ELLORA, INDIA, 8TH CENTURY A.D.

THE KAILASA TEMPLE, it is safe to say, is one of the most astonishing "buildings" in the history of architecture. This shrine was not constructed of stone on stone, it was in fact not constructed at all: it was carved, sculpted in toto from the volcanic hillside! A squared, U-shaped trench was first cut into the slope to a depth of close to 100 feet. The "liberated" mass in the center was then patiently carved from the living rock to produce a freestanding, two-story Hindu temple of dazzling complexity. The temple, which is dedicated to Shiva, the oft-threatening god of the Hindu trilogy, measures 109 feet wide by 164 feet long. It stands on an elevated plinth to attain greater presence in its tight surroundings. The complex consists of entry, Nandi (i.e., bull) shrine, open porch, main hall, and inner sanctum. Variously scaled panels, friezes, and sculpture highlight many surfaces.

An estimated 200,000 tons of rock were excavated to create the Kailasa Temple, and some historians point out that it would have been less costly and time-consuming to have constructed the temple from the ground up. As built, it reputedly took almost a hundred years to finish—using 1-inch chisels! It is thought that the temple originally had a white stucco finish that brightened the overall effect, while also symbolizing the snow-covered peaks of the gods' home in the Himalayas.

The late Percy Brown, whose two-volume *Indian Architecture* is indispensable to any study of Indian culture, sums up the shrine thus: "The temple of Kailasa at Ellora is not only the most stupendous single work of art executed in India, but as an example of rock-architecture it is unrivalled. . . . The Kailasa is an illustration of one of those rare occasions when men's minds, hearts, and hands work in unison towards the consummation of a supreme ideal."

LINGARAJ TEMPLE
BHUBANESWAR, INDIA, 11TH CENTURY

HINDU RELIGIOUS ARCHITECTURE should be approached while keeping its symbolic intentions in mind, not our esthetic parochialism. The temple is totemistic, a religious experience before an esthetic one: the Hindu in front of his shrine sees a cosmic diagram, the Westerner merely a fascinating building. Often, as here, a mountain of stone, the temple forms an abode for the god and is itself an object of devotion. A religious Hindu might leave a daily flower or offering at the temple, but he prays to his family deity at his own shrine at home, the parish priest at the temple performing *puja* (worship) on behalf of his flock. Group celebrations and sacred dances do take place at the temple, but in the *mandapas,* or pillared halls, attached to the shrine.

Theoretically, all design facets of the temple—outside and in, from site selection to finials—are governed by an elaborate set of ancient rules and geometric proportions called the *shilpa shastras.* Though appearance is, of course, important, design is generated more by ritual and mathematical iconography. The basic temple form is often besieged by a reluctance to leave any space unattended, resulting in a complexity and richness of decorative sculpture elsewhere unknown—a "vegetative abundance," wrote Tillich. Such rigid systemization might constitute a straitjacket if it were not for those glorious interpreters of this inheritance: the Indian architects and sculptors. The manner in which these men of genius worked and the technical bravura with which they achieved their results provide us with some of architecture's masterpieces.

At Bhubaneswar, 270 miles south of Calcutta, we find one of India's legendary centers of Hindu temple architecture (the other is Khajuraho; see p. 42). By the eleventh century, this holy area reputedly had over seven thousand shrines casually disposed around its sacred lake. Today a clutch of temples remain and are lovingly tended, with several hundred remnants nearby. Chief of these is the Lingaraj, or Great Temple, which rises in a walled compound 520 feet long, with over a hundred small shrines around it, all closed to non-Hindus. The complex dates basically from around A.D. 1000—the beginning of the Romanesque in Europe.

The temple's limestone *vimana,* or sanctuary (*background, right*), rises to a height of 180 feet and is entered by a pyramidal *jagamohan,* or anteroom (*left*). The *vimana* is squarish in plan and wrapped in clustered bands that vertically bend inward to make an overall tapered profile. The juncture of *vimana* with *jagamohan* is not as adroit as one might wish—they simply abut each other rather impolitely—but the complex is intriguing. Note the prominent undercutting of layers throughout, to create shadow lines and keep monsoon rains off the walls. The strata in the *vimana* are enriched at every sixth tier, while the pancaked layers of the *jagamohan* diminish in thickness as they rise, carrying astounding tiny bands of sculpted elephants, soldiers, and such. "Air sculpture," boldly outlined against the sky, and heraldic medallions enliven both buildings and punctuate the interactions of horizontal and vertical. The modest shrines in the foreground of the photograph give a leapfrog buildup of scale to the whole (as does the figure at lower left).

The West needs to know more—much more—of India's extraordinary architectural contributions: they could richly expand our horizons.

KANDARIYA MAHADEVA TEMPLE

KHAJURAHO, INDIA, C. 1030

THE KANDARIYA TEMPLE epitomizes India's glorious period of religious building, an era which in north central India spanned the eleventh and twelfth centuries. (In southern India a vigorous spate of temple building lasted until the seventeenth century, but quality gradually gave way to unimaginative conformity.) The Kandariya's scale buildup, superb profile, and ferment of sculpted surfaces establish it in a very special niche.

Resting on an elevated podium, the temple (*right*) proceeds to establish a crisscross of interwoven horizontals and verticals. The lower part consists of lateral bands, few of them the same height, stepping back as they rise and with proper profile, to provide a base for the temple itself. Vertical clusters of figures stand at angles to this base to probe upward, eventually melding with the stepped "pyramids" at the top. The temple culminates in the well-scaled *shikara* (tower), its profile recalling Mount Meru, the home of the gods. It is building become sculpture.

The interior is approached by a humbling flight of stairs that delivers one to the open *mandapa*, or columned hall, then to a closed *mandapa* with ritual dance platform, and finally to the *garbhagriha*, or sanctuary, where rests the *lingam*, the phallic symbol of Shiva. It is a progression of light into darkness. An outer passage with five balconies (two visible in the photograph) surrounds this core.

It should be kept in mind that interior space in Indian temples plays—has to play—a minor role. Since the temples were constructed solely of masonry (no wood-trussed roofs), with no utilization of vaulting, large spans of stone were impossible.

The famous erotic panels of the Khajuraho temples—there are over a dozen major ones—attain an ultimate at the Kandariya (*opposite*). Sexuality was an uninhibited celebration of life, and its unabashed depiction simply a document of the life process.

THE ABBEY OF POMPOSA

ITALY, 9TH–12TH CENTURY A.D.

FOLLOWING THE FALL of Rome in 476, then centuries of appalling nothingness—until Charlemagne—Europe stirred apprehensively as the Millennium year 1000 approached. That milestone safely passed, most of Western Europe awoke politically and culturally.

The architecture—almost all ecclesiastic—that then began to take root is called the Romanesque, though little of ancient Rome will be seen except columns and capitals. Heavy-walled and small-windowed, their longitudinal plans ending with a semicircular apse, Romanesque churches evolved with imagination and national variations over much of Europe. The earlier churches were roofed with wood trusses, the later with stone vaults.

One of the most appealing Italian churches of the period is the Abbey of Pomposa, begun in the late ninth century on marshy land 50 miles southeast of Ferrara. Becoming popular with local dignitaries—including the Benedictine monk and musical reformer Guido d'Arezzo—the church was extended some 26 feet in the eleventh and twelfth centuries. By the late thirteenth century, however, the area had to be abandoned because of malaria. Today, with drainage and mosquito control, the province is healthy but intriguingly lost in a *grande solitudine*.

The interior of the three-aisle abbey is architecturally simple, with planar, almost shaved stone walls—note that there are no moldings—topped by a wood-truss roof. The raised sanctuary level in the apse is the only structural accent. This purposeful simplicity provides the perfect background for the extraordinary frescoes that cover almost all available wall space. Painted in the 1350s by Iacopo da Bologna, they combine medieval primitiveness with Byzantine overtones—accents from nearby Ravenna. The walls depict Old and New Testament scenes; the apse shows Christ with the Blessed. Superb.

CATHEDRAL OF SAN SALVADOR

AVILA, SPAIN, BEGUN 1091

AVILA, THE HIGHEST town in Spain and a former Roman outpost, is among that country's most picturesque cities. Handsomely perched on the Sierra de Gredos, it epitomizes the medieval, with its massive town wall punctuated by eighty-six towers topped by endless crenelations. The granite wall was erected (1090–99) against the Moors and the perils of centuries of war and strife. The city contains several first-rate Romanesque churches and the Cathedral of San Salvador (*opposite*).

The church, though begun in the Romanesque style, evolved through the years into the basic Gothic form seen today. Its recessed portal combines both styles, with a round-headed Romanesque door set in Gothic pointed arches. The entry, with its panel of thirteenth-century saints above and unusual sculpture at the top, all tightly framed by buttresses, hints of a Moorish influence: an elaborate access surrounded by simple flanking walls. Gothic crockets enliven the starkness. The lofty interior is noted more for its details (retable, two wrought-iron pulpits) than for its Gothic correctness.

The overall atmosphere of church and town evokes an unspoiled, long-ago era.

SAN ZENO MAGGIORE

VERONA, ITALY, 1120–38

SAN ZENO, THOUGH too little visited, is rewarding outside and in. Facing an open piazza and cradled between a well-turned campanile (1178) and a haphazard but apparently habitable ancient tower (fourteenth century), its tufa

facade asserts a sharp geometry with a quietly stated verticality (*left*). Note that it is subdivided by narrow pilasters—a line of tiny arches in between—and given accents by the large rose window and the projecting, trimly arched porch. The north wall, on the other hand, stresses the horizontal—such dichotomy in the Middle Ages was not uncommon—its alternating bands of light and dark stone finding a congenial echo in the campanile. This Romanesque church is the fifth on the site, earlier ones having been destroyed by fire or man or having been outgrown. Part of the present interior dates from a fourteenth-century expansion, when a colorful Gothic keel-shaped ceiling of painted wood was installed.

But felicitous though they may be, the exterior and interior of San Zeno bow to the absolutely glorious bronze panels on the two front doors (1138; *opposite*). Depicting deeds from the Old and the New Testament plus scenes from allegorical tales, these forty-eight panels revel in their "barbaric" primitiveness. Sculpted by an artist named Nicolò, with help from an assistant known as Guglielmo, the panels proclaim their message with astounding vigor. (Nicolò also carved the sixteen larger scale stone bas-relief panels on either side and the angry griffins on which the porch columns rest.)

A unique facet of medieval Italian sculpture, the San Zeno figures leap from the panels with a conviction that every sinner must confront on entering the church.

THE TEMPLE CITY OF ANGKOR WAT

THE TEMPLE-TOMB complex of Angkor Wat, erected by Suryavarman II (r. 1113–50), is one of the most remarkable in existence. It boasts an unprecedented layout (measuring 4,250 feet by 5,000 feet), contains a towering buildup of masses, and unfolds an almost endless sculpted frieze—yet it is the least known of the world's shrines. Located on a branch of the Mekong River long claimed by the jungle, the Angkor area was "discovered" only in 1858 when Henri Mouhot, an intrepid French naturalist, first saw its vine-smothered ruins. Beginning early in this century, these unbelievable remains were carefully unshackled from trees and undergrowth and stabilized by French archaeologists, a process not basically completed until the 1920s.

Angkor's overall layout was originally enclosed by a vast wall (now almost completely vanished) within which was a wide moat embracing the entire temple compound. Through a propylaea (entry; *opposite, left*) one traverses a lengthy causeway to the outermost of three walled, nearly square palisades that enclose the temple area proper. Continuing past courtyards containing two libraries and places for meditation, one arrives at the innermost sanctum, resting on a high podium and reached by challengingly steep stairs reminiscent of those in Mayan temples. An elaborately layered, unmortared stone tower crowns the center, rising to a height of 213 feet, with similar but slightly lower towers in each corner. Their sovereign profile is memorable.

Although the temple is dedicated to the Indian god Vishnu—Indian religion was then of great importance in Cambodia—there is little of the Hindu casualness in site planning here. All is axial-symmetrical and oriented on the cardinal compass points, with cosmology always in the background. There is, however, no rigidity in Angkor's spaces—open or closed—but an exciting bristle of angles, heights, and interactions, quickened by almost constant changes of level. The courtyard spaces are alive. (It should be added that inasmuch as the temple's rooms are roofed with stone beams of limited structural capacity, or with corbelled arches, whose layers step inward as they rise, the interior spaces are not nearly as imposing.)

Angkor Wat was a religious compound and sepulchre for the god-king of a scope never seen before or after. Of unknown architect, this high point of Khmer culture was abandoned in 1431, when the area fell to the Thais.

As Osbert Sitwell, the English critic, summed it up: "Let it be said immediately that Angkor, as it stands, ranks as a chief wonder of the world, one of the summits to which human genius has aspired in stone."

CHARTRES CATHEDRAL

FRANCE, 1195–1220

THE EXTRAORDINARY efflorescence in twelfth- and thirteenth-century France of what came to be known as the Gothic ushered in a triumphant period in the history of architecture. It was an era in which religious fervor and the building of unparalleled churches swept Europe for some four hundred years. Gothic churches fused architecture, engineering, and art into glorious celebrations, creating magnificent houses of God.

Gothic architecture was not merely a new "style": it was the culmination of a structural revolution that enabled its architects, via rib vaulting and buttressing, to conquer unprecedented spaces. Moreover, in many respects it grew from the inside out. The Gothic's characteristic pointed arch vaulting could span naves hitherto impossible with round-headed vaults, while its architects' search for ever-greater heights pushed stone engineering to the limit. (The reach of the nave at Beauvais was so great that it partially collapsed in 1284.) With ribs carrying the concentrated load of the roof onto buttresses, the outer wall of the church became liberated, making "glass walls" feasible and thus giving rise to the Gothic's famous stained glass. (Compare the Romanesque's near-solid walls and small windows.) As churches grew wider and loftier, it became more complex to transfer the weight of the roof to the ground, a problem which was resolved by the famous flying buttresses. On the interior an atmosphere of airiness and luminosity resulted, with a cadence of bay divisions, marked by ribs, producing a rhythm that climaxed with the apsidal sanctuary.

It should be kept in mind that not all medieval churches are architecturally successful; of perhaps a hundred in France, only a dozen or so are notable. Moreover, the Gothic was ill regarded by the time of the Renaissance: compared to the Classic, it seemed anarchic, and even the great Christopher Wren deplored its "Rudeness." (It was, of course, absurdly named for a tribe of barbarians.) Today most of us find Gothic architecture's soaring naves and aerial buttresses breathtaking, its sculpture spiritual, and the richness of its stained glass dazzling.

Chartres Cathedral was partially built on the foundations of a previous church, most of which burned in 1194, leaving an awkward—and only partially resolved—problem of how to incorporate the old facade, which had survived. Rebuilding commenced at once, and by 1220 (an extraordinarily short time) the church was largely finished. Like all French cathedrals (as opposed to the generally edge-of-town English ones), Chartres partakes of, indeed dominates, the community that picturesquely enfolds it (*below*). As with almost all churches of its day, it served a spectrum of medieval civic needs—not unlike eighteenth-century New England meeting houses.

The exterior of Chartres rejoices in some of the finest religious sculpture to be seen anywhere. Though the sculpture in the triple-arched main entry, the Royal Doorway, lacks a proper architectural frame, the porticos on the north and south are magnificent. Above, the flying buttresses pull the eye. From the outside walkway of the high midriff of the church (*opposite*), one intimately grasps the adventurous stone engineering that made the Gothic cathedrals possible: it was a quantum leap. On the inside, Chartres's luminous thirteenth-century stained glass ranks among its glories: its biblical illustrations doubled as books for a basically illiterate congregation.

With Gothic's daringly innovative structure, sculpture of almost mystic intensity, and stained glass that opened a new world of art, it is little wonder that the style is so richly rewarding. Its cathedrals might be said to be symbols of heaven.

ROUND CHURCH
HAGBY, SWEDEN, LATE 1200S

SWEDEN HAS LONG favored a clean, geometric statement in its architecture: here in this ancient church we find cylinder, cone, and triangle in apposition. The geometry is further emphasized by the contrast of whitewashed stone walls and pitch-blackened wood shingles. The freestanding bell tower—also stained black—sets up a spatial tension with the body of the church, while the play of its sinewy "sticks" counterpoints the church's sturdy mass. On the interior, the box pews of the circular nave focus on the rounded sanctuary, which projects at the rear.

TOWN AND CATHEDRAL
OF ORVIETO

ITALY, 1290–1500s

THE PLATEAU ON which the town and cathedral of Orvieto sit has been occupied since the Etruscans settled in the region more than eight thousand years ago. These little-known people, supposedly out of Asia—Herodotus mentions Lydia—and brushed by ancient Greek culture and language, established important city-states in the hills and plains north of the Tiber, attaining their greatest eminence in the sixth and fifth centuries B.C. They eventually succumbed to the Romans, and most of their cities (but not their fascinating tombs) were destroyed. Etruscan builders, incidentally, had considerable influence on Roman architecture, particularly in the development of the true arch.

Orvieto, with its base some 660 feet above the River Paglia and its sharply cut flanks giving it clarity, possesses one of Italy's most distinctive profiles (*right*). Though the town is full of historic buildings, none can equal its superb Romanesque-Gothic cathedral, begun in 1290, and the medieval square it faces. The startling use of black-and-white courses of marble on the flanks and interior of the church approaches the spectacular. This use of "color" constitutes a distinct Italian version of Gothic, as opposed to that seen in the cathedrals of northern Europe. One might say that the churches in Orvieto (and in Siena) achieve their magnificence by the use of color and decoration, while those in France, England, and Germany rely basically on structure for their effect. (There are no flying buttresses at Orvieto, for instance, for its roof is of wood.)

The front of the cathedral, which was not fully finished until the 1500s, sparkles with mosaics and sculpture, and when seen from a direct side elevation

(*opposite*), its "air sculpture" ensorcels one forward. Note the contrast of the boldly horizontal bands of marble wall with the rich verticality of the paneled edge of the facade, while the silhouette of sculpture acts as punctuation.

With the scene pacified by the quiet square in front, the overall effect is of an admirable urban and architectural cordiality.

HÄVERÖ CHURCH

UPPLAND, SWEDEN, C. 1300

MASONS HAVE OPTIONS in laying stone walls. At one extreme, there is
the cyclopean wall composed of gigantic boulders set without mortar, as in
Machu Picchu, Peru (c. 1500), where random-sized stones are so precisely
trimmed and laid up that a knife blade cannot penetrate their joints. At the other,
we find this appealing country church in central Sweden, where the mortar
statement is almost as important as the lithic. Built about 1300 (the vaulting
later), the Häverö Church magnificently employs local stone and mortar to
produce a wall that any age would relish. Note, too, that the massive stone finds
elegant polarity in the wiry wrought-iron gate. Masonry at its finest.

SAINT MARK'S SQUARE

VENICE, 9TH–19TH CENTURY

PEDESTRIANS IN OUR grid-bound cities rarely encounter spatial pulsations, surprise approaches, or unexpected three-dimensional pleasures, for few exist. More should. Our routine checkerboarding of square block after square block creates a city of tedious urban cores.

An exception to planning banality lies in front of Saint Mark's Cathedral in Venice. This regularly irregular, unsquare square is, many feel, the most exhilarating example of town planning and architecture to be seen anywhere. Napoleon, who himself had the square's west end properly finished (1810), said that "Saint Mark's is the most beautiful drawing room in Europe." Le Corbusier added, "Today Venice is still our teacher."

Among the square's most powerful impacts is the pedestrian approach from the west. Down a narrow, shop-lined sidewalk, one sees in the distance an arched opening with a promise of freedom beyond. As one draws nearer, the arch dominates and quickens the sharp perspective on the right, while a tower tantalizingly disappears upward. Then, with a step forward, there explodes a brilliant fusion of space, architecture, color, and sunshine (*opposite*). It is no casual introduction.

Saint Mark's Square evolved through the centuries, the first effort being a modest forecourt in front of the church (which was started in 829, then rebuilt in its Byzantine glory in 1063–94). The expansion of the square was, however, always carried out with respect to what had been there before. The pivotal campanile was begun in 888 and its design likewise matured through the years. On its collapse in 1902, donations from much of the world had it rebuilt precisely as it had been, but with greater internal bracing. Note that the campanile is freestanding from the building at the right to "announce" that the space continues around the corner, while also giving a hint of the Doge's Palace beyond. Although not apparent in the photograph, the whole square is arcaded to give sun and rain protection plus visual homogeneity. The campanile's verticality not only serves as the crucial fulcrum of the square, its architectural reticence counterpoints the luxuriance of the church. Bravissimo.

P O S I T A N O

A M A L F I C O A S T , I T A L Y

EXPLORED BY THE Greeks in the sixth century B.C. (see nearby Paestum, page 16), settled by the Romans, mauled by the Pisans (1135), and favored by sybarites ever since, the Amalfi Coast has miraculously survived in large measure intact. Positano is one of its jewels. Its mist-shrouded, rugged mountain backdrop is unharassed by man, its juncture with the sea is considerate. Its "architecture without architects" (Bernard Rudofsky) is respectful, its whitewashed, oft cubic forms echoing the Mediterranean vernacular. Nature and man hand in hand.

SEVILLE CATHEDRAL

SPAIN, 1402–1520

SEVILLE CATHEDRAL IS the largest Gothic church in the world, its size only later surpassed, in the Renaissance, by Saint Peter's in Rome. Though it shows influences from French Gothic prototypes (and possibly help from French architects) and from Italy (primarily Milan Cathedral), it carries a personality of its own. Its nave (*opposite*) is soaringly powerful, one of the too-little-appreciated Gothic glories of Europe.

The cathedral reputedly was constructed on the foundations of a mosque, thus producing an unusual squarish plan. In the resultant five-aisle church, the lofty nave is flanked by slightly lower double side-aisles, so that the towering central piers rise straight upward uncompromised, as it were, by the triforium gallery and clerestory that hem typical Gothic naves. Pausing only briefly for small decorative capitals, the nave piers meld with the clearly stated vault of the ceiling, topping off at 132 feet. (The nave of Chartres is 120 feet high.) Seville's breathtaking—and structurally daring—nave combines soaring verticality with the horizontal mystery of the side aisles. As perhaps can be grasped from the photograph, the effect is awesome.

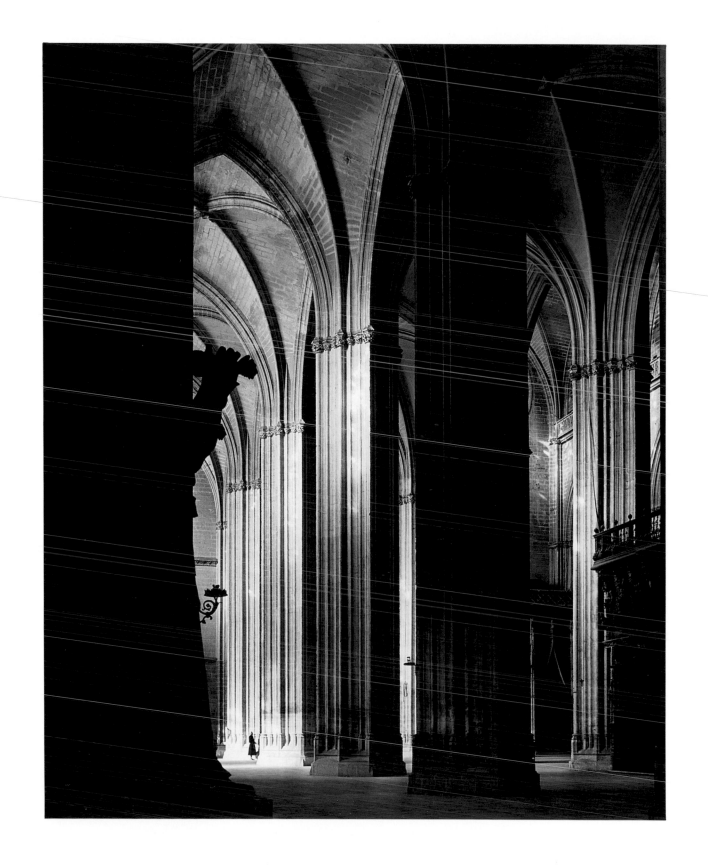

ARCADES AND FOUNTAINS

BERN, SWITZERLAND, 15TH–20TH CENTURY

THE OLD TOWN section of Bern forms one of Europe's fetching urban byways. Situated on an elevated point of land, with the River Aare wrapping around its peninsula, the area offered its settlers a sandstone rampart for a site, complete with river as moat. The town—founded in 1191—appreciated nature's beneficence, and one of the early structures was a castle on the promontory. Bern's hairpin topography led to a street pattern of three primary, roughly parallel streets, with lesser walks on the lower, river-edge flanks.

The buildings that eventually lined these streets evolved into a basic pattern of four stories in height—shops below, living quarters above—with continuous arcades (*Lauben*) running the length of each block to provide weather protection, shopping ease, and street integrity. Window boxes with seasonal flowers poke from most living rooms, while the curved eaves typical of Canton Bern overhang and protect the upper floor. Note, too, the use of slatted wood shutters. A civilized scale marks all.

To provide convenient water for man, beast, and fire, a series of fountains cheer these well-bred streets, the first fountain being built in the mid-thirteenth century. In a tradition that became a regional pride through the years, these water sources provided a socializing forum for each neighborhood. In the 1500s, the early wooden wells were replaced by stone fountains, generally with ornamental sculpture. A public Master of Fountains was even appointed. Then in the early 1800s "the fountains were looked upon chiefly as being hindrances to traffic," and most were removed, but fortunately put in storage. By 1891, on the city's seven hundredth anniversary, pride returned and the fountains we see today were completely restored. There are twenty major ones, the last of which dates from 1942. Most are highly competent works of civic art, some are amusing, all contribute to urban amenity.

The photograph opposite depicts the Junkerngasse (*left*), a fountain dating from the 1700s (*center*), and a flamboyant Gothic church dedicated to Saint Vincent (*right*). The church was begun in 1421, but not basically finished until 1573; the tower, spire, and crockets were not added until the end of the last century.

When Bern expanded—as it assumed a lead role in 1353 on joining the Swiss Confederation and was made the seat of government in 1848—its delightful peninsula, being "isolated," escaped most depradations. One of Europe's best-preserved towns, Bern was proclaimed a "world landmark" by UNESCO in 1983.

THE STROZZI PALACE

FLORENCE, 1489

THE PALAZZO, as a fifteenth-century mid-urban domicile, numbers among Florence's many architectural contributions. Formidable, virtually fortified, these stern palaces, rising abruptly from the sidewalks, are the Early Renaissance's somewhat arrogant versions of townhouses for the powerful. Chief among them is the Strozzi Palace by Benedetto da Maiano (1442–97) and Il Cronaca (1454–1508).

Strozzi's design culminates the Florentine palazzo "pattern," which favors a flat facade of three stories—each level marked by a prominent full-width stringcourse (horizontal banding)—topped by an outsize cornice (here, 7 feet high). Stone of almost theatrical rustication commands the facade, with semicircular arches crowning all the major openings. Note that the radiating voussoirs (wedge-shaped stones) of the arches increase in length as they rise to the keystone. Divided two-arched windows with varying ornamental panels are typical of the upper floors, while squarish windows mark the lower. A haughty main entrance (*opposite*) leads to a central courtyard.

This domestic impertinence was the product of a unique period of architectural searching, the Renaissance. Born—almost exploding—in one city, Florence, and at one time, the early 1400s, the Renaissance eventually influenced most of Europe. And in spite of its "rebirth" name, it was rarely a resuscitation of ancient prototypes, Roman or otherwise. One of its key forces was the rise of the middle class, the bourgeoisie, to counter the power of the clergy and the nobility (secular buildings eventually became more important than religious ones). Artistically, the Renaissance was spurred by the discovery of the laws of perspective, primarily by architect Filippo Brunelleschi about 1420; mathematics flourished. At the same time, Florence rose to meteoric commercial and financial prominence throughout Europe. The Renaissance ushered in a new level of civilized living, the beginning of humanism. As Burckhardt put it, Florence was "the first modern state in the world." Art and, of course, architecture responded.

KING'S COLLEGE CHAPEL

CAMBRIDGE, ENGLAND, 1446–1515

THERE ARE NO spatial surprises in King's College Chapel, for its open, rectangular interior space is immediately graspable. Yet this narrow, lofty, lengthy chapel is one of the great rooms in architecture. It radiates light: some two-thirds of each of its four walls are of stained glass, which fills all the space between the buttresses. The glass is not of a medieval richness but bright, with considerable clear or opaque panes (grisaille) setting off the figures. (The chapel, dating several hundred years after the High Gothic—and built for a distinguished university—did not need to have its stained glass serve as "book" for an unlettered congregation.) With the exception of the west window, which was designed in 1879, the glass dates from 1517–47 and was the work of a German-born and a Flemish artist.

This luminous interior, which measures 290 feet long by 40 feet wide, is presided over by a delicate spider web of vaulting. Its stone fans appear almost gossamer as they reach out from the walls to weave a mantle over the nave.

The pious Henry VI founded King's College in 1441, laid the foundation stone for the chapel five years later, and apparently issued specifications for its design. However, no specific overall architect is known. Henry James considered the chapel the culmination of English Perpendicular Gothic architecture and in 1879 termed it "one of the noblest."

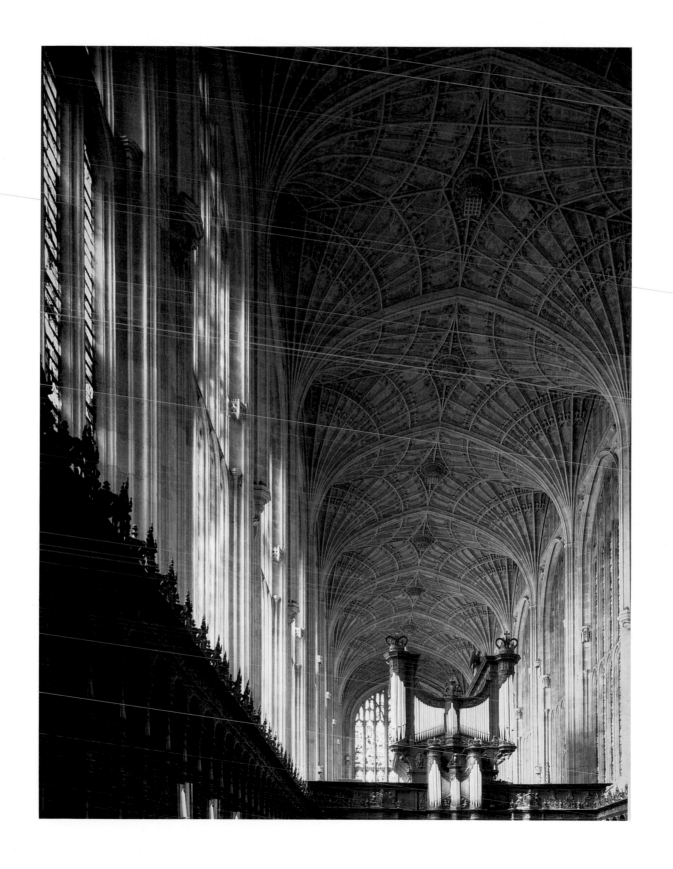

THE DOME OF SAINT PETER'S

ROME'S MAGISTERIAL Saint Peter's did not spring full blown: it required the brilliance of a dozen distinguished architects 174 years (1452–1626) to complete. Chief among them were Donato Bramante, one of the great architects of the High Renaissance, who proposed the church's basic plan—a Greek cross topped by a dome—and Michelangelo Buonarroti, who carried out Bramante's plan after the latter's death, while greatly simplifying and strengthening the earlier design. Michelangelo then concentrated his attention on the mighty dome for which he is so well known.

Influenced by Brunelleschi's dome atop Santa Maria del Fiore (1434) in Florence, Michelangelo's proposal called for a hemispheric shape. However, after Michelangelo's death in 1564, the work was finished (1591) by Giacomo della Porta, who added to the dome's overall height. The four small companion domes were designed by Giacomo Vignola. An expansion of the nave in 1603 to accommodate the growing congregation pushed the facade forward and unfortunately inhibited a proper view of Michelangelo's noble crown from Gianlorenzo Bernini's piazza, the main approach to the church.

Although this middle view is unsatisfactory, the dome from a distance caps the building with aplomb, while from the terrace level of the church itself (*opposite*), the scale buildup is masterful. Note the scale progression from the small dome at the right, to the medium one atop the corner pavilion at the left, to the drum and base of the great dome beyond. Their geometric interplay contributes to the overall excitement. Note, too, the vigorous plasticity of these elements and their three-dimensional vitality. (The silhouetted figures give an index of size.) The stalwartly projected pairs of columns encircling the drum form part of the buttress system, which continues upward as ribs of the dome.

On the interior, the dome soars 390 feet above the floor—and above Bernini's incomparable Baroque baldachino (1633; *right, foreground*). The dome, the diameter of which is 138 feet, is of brick, closely double-hulled for strength and higher exterior profile. (Four belts of iron chains were found necessary for structural support.) The coupled columns seen on the exterior of the drum are repeated within as pilasters flanking the windows, which flood the nave with light. The sixteen ribs that lead to the cupola act as frames for the rows of mosaics by Giuseppe Cesari (1568–1640). In the pendentives supporting the dome are prominent circular mosaics of the four Evangelists. Note, too, the elaborately framed panels of the vaults over the aisles, much of this decorative work taking place under Bernini.

Michelangelo's dome turned mathematics into sculpture, creating a scale in building of a new dimension, while producing as powerful an architectural encounter as one is apt to experience.

THE ESCORIAL

LIKE KING PHILIP II (1527–98), who commissioned it, much of the Escorial is imperious, ascetic—and dry. It stands aloof from the exciting heritage of Spanish architecture, in which the play of light, an oft-rambunctious ornamentation, and the visually unexpected can overflow. Haughty on its entrance facade (*opposite*), it becomes monotonous on its flanks, with endless unrelieved windows (one source says 2,673 of them) punched in the walls.

This colossal monastery, church, palace, country residence, college, mausoleum—the Real Monasterio de San Lorenzo del Escorial—is, nonetheless, one of Europe's major buildings. Located on a desolate rise some 30 miles from Madrid—and thus curiously detached from the capital—the granite complex was begun under architect Juan Bautista de Toledo, who died four years later and was succeeded by the more formal Juan de Herrera. Both men, it is pertinent to note, had worked in Italy, and the influence of the Late Renaissance can be seen here. King Philip was also intimately involved with its design, working closely with the architects, excising the ostentatious, and selecting many of the artists to embellish it. (Much of its painting and sculpture collection is outstanding.)

The entrance, topped by a statue of San Lorenzo, opens onto the Patio de los Reyes, with the icy facade of the enormous church directly on axis. The Patio de los Evangelistas occupies the right rear corner of the immense rectangular plan, the palace that to the left. The various divisions are separated by courtyards, sixteen in number. King Philip's own quarters are spartan.

Spain's riches from the New World and from the Philippines, which were named for Philip, paid for the building. The 1557 victory over the French army at Saint-Quentin prompted it.

Palazzo Chiericati

Vicenza, Italy, 1557

Andrea Palladio (1508–80) of Padua, Italy, is among the most imitated architects in history. His famous tripartite "Palladian window," with arched center section flanked by shorter rectangular openings, is—four hundred years after his death—a cliché of today's so-called Post-Modernism. However, both Bramante and Serlio used this motif earlier, the Italians calling it a Serliana. Hadrian's Temple at Ephesus (A.D. 118) might also have been of inspiration.

In the Palazzo Chiericati, Palladio opened new directions of civility in Late Renaissance domestic architecture. Occupying a refreshingly open site on the edge of this medieval town, just a short distance from his Teatro Olimpico (see page 78), it has been used for the public Museo Civico since 1855.

There is a mathematical organization and a cadence of modules in the Palazzo Chiericati that tie together the facade's plus-minus reciprocity of solids and voids. The central bay—with its tiny projection—is solid on the upper floor, the porches on either side are void, while a continuous open arcade runs the entire length of the ground floor. (In a curiously modern exchange, Signor Chiericati got 13 feet ceded to him by the city for keeping the arcade-walkway open to the public.) The whole is then strapped together by the bold edge-to-edge entablature, assisted by the row of balusters above. Note that the columns, Ionic above, Tuscan below, are doubled at the ends of the central bay.

One of the palazzo's piquant details is the row of statues and urns outlining the eave, a single one over each column, two over the doubled ones. These sculptures undoubtedly were inspired by those which Jacopo Sansovino placed atop his library (1540) in Venice. Sansovino's, in turn, might well have been prompted by the lively parade of figures around the circular periphery of Hadrian's Tomb (A.D. 139) in Rome. Incidentally, Palladio later used similar dancing figures *inside* his Teatro Olimpico.

ANDREA PALLADIO

TEATRO OLIMPICO

VICENZA, ITALY, 1584

PALLADIO'S TEATRO OLIMPICO is an outstanding example of the
High Renaissance, its interior, in particular, being of unexpected richness. At the
rear (*opposite*), the thirteen tiers of seats erupt vertically to vanish into a painted
heaven; they are escorted en route by a parade of local academicians.

The elaborately paneled two-story stage wall, with its profusion of possibly
distracting elements, is dominated by the large arched opening in the center, with
smaller entries on the sides, each revealing a sharp false perspective. In designing
the theater, Palladio drew upon ancient Roman prototypes and Vitruvius's ten
seminal books on architecture (46–30 B.C.). The fixed scenery of the theater was
finished after Palladio's death by Vicenzo Scamozzi.

The building remains to this day a monument of and to the Renaissance in its
freshness and theatricality.

Segovia and Its Inheritance

SPAIN: THE ALCAZAR, 11TH–15TH CENTURY; THE CATHEDRAL, 1522–77

SEGOVIA SYNTHESIZES the Spanish heritage of notable buildings intimate with their settings. Its famous aqueduct, the largest Roman construction in Spain and still in use, sets a proud counterpoint to the city's streets, which now crisscross its base. Trajan, the emperor who had a hand in the aqueduct's restoration, was himself born in Spain (about A.D. 53), and would have applauded this easy polarity.

The Alcazar (*left*) commands a strategic outcropping of the city's plateau high above the juncture of two small rivers. It is, of course, everyone's personal castle in Spain. Built in the eleventh century and rebuilt in the early fifteenth, it has a dashing, even romantic intimacy with its site that is difficult to equal. Muslim influence is seen in the name and in the building itself, particularly the interior.

Segovia's Late Gothic cathedral (*opposite*) gathers the town about it close up, while establishing a prominent and dramatic urban profile from a distance. Its 295-foot-high tower, though reduced from an earlier one for structural reasons, still impresses. Begun in 1522, the church was completed in 1591 to a design by Juan Gil de Hontañón, but finished after his death by his highly talented son, Rodrigo Gil de Hontañón. Its three-aisle plan comprises a compact, rectangular nave, cell-like side chapels, and a semicircular apse. It is the last built of the great Gothic churches of Europe.

Segovia in many respects is a dream city: its architecture-site relations, fortuitous or planned, have lessons for us all.

CITY OF FATEHPUR SIKRI

INDIA, 1571–85

THERE ARE NOT MANY "instant cities" in this world, and the most intriguing by far is India's Fatehpur Sikri. The Emperor Akbar (1542–1605), an exceptionally enlightened Moghul ruler, reputedly had long and in vain wanted a son and heir. When advised to consult a holy man in a village west of his capital at Agra, Akbar journeyed forth, made his obeisance, explained his problem, and in due course fathered three sons. As a tribute to the saint, Salim ed-Din Chishti, and to his village, the emperor commissioned this extraordinary on-the-site city for his new capital.

Straddling a sandstone ridge, with a lake (now dry) at its feet, Fatehpur Sikri (City of Victory) was begun in 1571 and finished fourteen years later. Although the city served as the palace-capital, it is doubtful that all the administrative infrastructure—let alone the dwellings for lesser nobles and retainers—was ever completely accommodated locally. There is still ambiguity among scholars concerning the size and extent of its working population—and its housing—on the plateau and off.

The mere fact of Fatehpur's "instant" completion is, of course, prodigious but more impressive to us today are the quality, scale, and diversity of its buildings and the spaces they define. For here is no routine grid of mindless squares, but a series of pulsating urban spaces defined by polite structures. Yet Fatehpur is more successful as a series of vistas and specific spatial encounters than as an overall triumph of urbanism. Its parts are better than the whole: it lacks, for instance, an orienting spine.

Fatehpur's fresh and innovative architecture, with its vast array of building types, represents—like most Moghul building—a fusion of Indian and Islamic cultures. The underlying structure is generally of Hindu post-and-beams, in many cases roofed with Muslim vaults and domes. All is carried out here with cohesive and sympathetic scale: note the "neighborhood" atmosphere.

The terrace in the midground of the photograph is a *pachisi* court. Laid out in marble squares, the "Royal Game of India" was played with slave girls directed by dice thrown by the emperor and nobles, who stood in the five-story pavilion—the Panch Mahal—at right. Though it is not specifically known what the victors' or victims' pleasures were, we still enjoy our version of the game four centuries later.

Akbar used Fatehpur Sikri as his capital for relatively few years, military and related affairs in northwest India demanding his presence, and (puzzlingly) he spent the last ten years of his life back in Agra. After the emperor's departure, Fatehpur was largely deserted, but fortunately never heavily vandalized or destroyed. It was not "rediscovered" until the early years of the last century.

JOHN WHIPPLE HOUSE

IPSWICH, MASSACHUSETTS, C. 1640, 1670, 1720

THE SEVENTEENTH- TO eighteenth-century wooden houses of New England form a unique chapter in the architectural heritage of the United States. Indeed, so appealing are these so-called "Cape Cod" houses that they are still one of suburbia's favored types, although sometimes far removed from their original culture.

Wood was, of course, the favored building material, since probably ninety percent of the settlers in the 1600s were yeomen who had to clear their land before farming could commence. Thus, in effect, building material was free. Wood was also easily worked and offered good insulation, an important factor in the long New England winters. By the mid-seventeenth century, New England sawmills were even exporting clapboards to the mother country.

We find in the Whipple House one of the finest early wooden dwellings in the United States, a hoary gem which underwent several expansions and many vicissitudes before being rescued late in the last century. The oldest part of the house (*opposite, left*) consists of a "hall," i.e., family room–kitchen, facing an enormous fireplace. Two bedrooms fill the second floor, with another bedroom under the eaves. Construction is based on heavy oak framing, mortised and tenoned together, then enclosed by clapboards left unpainted. The interior is plastered for looks and against drafts. Casement windows with tiny diamond panes provide reasonable daylight.

About thirty years after the first section was built, a large addition was attached at the right, making the house approximately 45 feet long by 16 feet deep. Then, some fifty years later, a lean-to ell, containing a proper kitchen and another bedroom, was attached at the rear. Note the house's stretched-out front, which almost automatically indicates that it was expanded. Note, too, the prominent triangular gables high-pitched against snow, the enormous central chimney for both cooking and heating, the thin clapboards, and the small medieval windows (using the largest panes then available)—all are indices of the earliest domestic architecture in New England.

By the end of the last century, the Whipple House was in an appalling condition, but in 1898 it was purchased by the Ipswich Historical Society, moved to this site from nearby, and beautifully restored. In the 1950s the adjacent garden was planted with the typical herbs used at the time for medicinal remedies, dyes, seasonings, and such (seventeenth-century home gardens were primarily utilitarian). Today all is in splendid shape. We need such echoes of the past: they are touchstones, no matter where they may be.

TAJ MAHAL

AGRA, INDIA, 1643

MUCH OF HISTORY'S funerary architecture varies from the egregious to the doleful. However, India's Taj Mahal, built by Emperor Shah Jahan for his favorite wife, radiates love, beauty, and serenity. It is the tomb of Mumtaz Mahal (Jewel of the Palace), who died giving birth to her fourteenth child. The Shah, the fifth Moghul emperor, was buried at her side in 1666.

The approach to the Taj—at right angles to its axis—was carefully calculated to begin with a wide, tree-lined promenade, climaxed by a stately gatehouse at the end. Through the entry pavilion's purposely constricted arched opening, one gets a glimpse of bright, faraway domes. One passes through the red stone entry to unexpectedly discover a veritable explosion of vistas, with the white marble Taj distantly shining in the sun. The progression of horizontal open promenade, tight somber gateway, and unfolding panorama combine with vertical spaces of steps down, a garden, and a teasingly raised fountain to generate spatial magic. It has been called a passage "from the profane to the sacred" (Alistair Sherer). The contrast of materials—red stone entry with white marble tomb—is also part of the architect's cunning.

The tomb rests serenely on an elevated white marble platform, 313 feet square, and is "protected" by four minarets that create vertical accents and spatial interplay. The Hindu-inspired cupolas (*chhatris*) of the minarets establish kinship with their counterparts flanking the great dome—the Dome of Heaven—knitting all together. The tomb itself is also square in plan, but its corners are chamfered to create three-dimensionality and thus to encourage circumambulation. It measures 186 feet on a side, with its overall height equal to its width; the dome towers 200 feet above the platform. The lofty height of the rectangular frame of the entrance equals half the width of the whole structure.

The Taj's terrace platform is lined with panels of small Moghul arches; their repetition of the various arched openings of the building itself, culminating in the entry, develops an imposing homogeneity. Khoranic inscriptions and exquisitely inlaid mosaic flowers outline each element.

Though no single architect for the Taj is known, Shah Jahan's own architect, as well as a Persian from Shiraz and a Turk named Afandi, are all mentioned as contributors, with the Shah himself playing a decisive role. Whoever the authors, their careful calculation paradoxically produces a work of great poetry—the most sorcerous building in the world.

SAN CARLO ALLE QUATTRO FONTANE

ROME, 1638–67

THE DEVELOPMENT IN the seventeenth to early eighteenth century of the Baroque movement gave architecture an exploratory new dimension, a liberation that freed it from the straight-line planar facades of the Renaissance. The curve became generator—in plan, section, and elevation. It might be said that architecture exploded and that the box of the previous century was dead. Moreover, the Baroque married the art of building to the arts of painting and sculpture more intimately than ever previously imagined. That this path to a new infinity had parallels with the burgeoning of science was no accident.

Beginning in Rome with Gianlorenzo Bernini (1598–1680) and Francesco Borromini (1599–1667)—genius rivals—the Baroque soon spread over most of western Europe, climaxing, with distinct variations, in South German Baroque and, in the New World, in Spain's Mexican outpost, where it erupted with a startling lack of architectural inhibition. Like all "styles," the Baroque ran its course: when the new fashion of the Greek Revival became popular in the last half of the eighteenth century, the Baroque phased out. For most of the more conservative nineteenth and early twentieth centuries, it was, indeed, regarded with suspicion if not disdain.

Borromini's San Carlo was begun in 1638 and was semifinished, without its facade, three years later, the money having run out. The church was not completed until 1667, the year of Borromini's tragic suicide. As perhaps can be grasped from the photograph, the restless, compacted two-tiered facade engages in a vigorous confrontation with the street. The church's three bays of curves and countercurves—emphasized by the bold sweep of the entablature—the side niches receding with statues, the center advancing with the saint, the two sizes of columns giving scale and frame, all make the front quiver. These rewards continue in the sculpted interior, where a fiendishly coffered dome presides over apses, squinches, pediments, and plaques with spatial delirium.

That so much intricately coordinated churning could be achieved in so little space epitomizes the Baroque.

THE TURKISH MOSQUE

DJERBA, TUNISIA, TRADITIONAL

HOMER'S LOTOPHAGI WERE AMONG the earliest to discover the charms of Djerba, some, indeed, being so taken with eating its lotus leaves — and enjoying the dulcet life — that Odysseus had to dragoon them to sail his boats back to Greece. The island today is not what it used to be, having been invaded by unsympathetic hotels, but traces of its ancient allure still can be found.

Though Berbers formed the basic native population through the centuries, Normans from Sicily, Spaniards, and Turks all wrestled for Djerba in the Middle Ages, the Turks ending in control (after 1574). The long Turkish occupation of Djerba left an architectural heritage of small-scale mosques unlike any in the world in their vernacular "innocence." The Turkish Mosque is a graphic example of what might be called homespun solid geometry. Cube, hemisphere, cylinder, cone — has architecture ever been so Euclidean?

Throughout this 17-mile-long island, there are other mosques whose "primitive" designers have produced some of the most sophisticated buildings to be seen in the Mediterranean.

SINDONE CHAPEL

TURIN, 1667–90

GUARINO GUARINI (1624–83), born in Modena, took the High Baroque to dazzling adventures in his adopted city of Turin. His Cappella della Santissima Sindone deftly lifted dome architecture to heights of ingenious imagination. The solid sphere of past cultures was transformed to a light-pierced, mathematical webbing of spaces. The dome interior (*opposite*) rises from a circular drum lined with six outsized windows that alternate with pedimented niches. Above leaps a crosshatching of ribs laid in diminishing hexagons, each "layer" resting on the midpoint of the one below. A twelve-sided star at the top radiates light from the lantern, a dove quietly in the center. Although the overall height of the dome is modest, the cunningly contrived foreshortening gives the interior tantalizing space.

Guarini, like many architects of his time, was highly skilled in geometry: his genius achieved a new dimension in this chapel where, as Rudolf Wittkower succinctly put it, his "daring diaphanous dome . . . turned over a new leaf of architectural history."

SAINT PAUL'S CATHEDRAL

THE DOME OF Saint Paul's has been described as "one of the most perfect in the world" (Pevsner). Moreover, it sits atop one of history's great churches. If the church's exterior asserts power and its interior seems more secular than dedicatedly spiritual, this is undoubtedly what Charles II, the monarch who commissioned it, wanted.

Sir Christopher Wren (1632–1723)—at age twenty-nine a Professor of Astronomy at Oxford—designed fifty-two churches in London after the Great Fire of 1666 wiped out most of the previous ones, along with the center of the city. Many of Wren's small churches are intimate, often charming, and always dextrous, but Saint Paul's had to be a monument to empire as well as a house of God. In this Wren succeeded admirably, a trip to Paris (1665–66) honing his wits, particularly as regards splendor and domes. (As can be seen in the photograph, Wren was also taken with the widely spaced, doubled Corinthian columns on the east front of the Louvre, which was nearing completion at the time of his visit.)

Saint Paul's assertive Late Renaissance facade—topped by two almost Baroque towers (one with bells, the other with a clock) and climaxed by the regal dome— sets an authoritative presence in London's crowded streets. (Unfortunately, Nicholas Hawksmoor's brilliant plan for a stately urban setting for the cathedral was never carried out.) The sculpture in the pediment depicts the conversion of Saint Paul. The dome rises 366 feet (with lantern) above the pavement: note the family resemblance of its lantern with the front towers, and the dome's correspondence with the towers. Michelangelo's dome atop Saint Peter's in Rome (see page 72), built a century earlier, was obviously an influence.

Lead-covered on a timber frame, the dome rests on a window-circled drum surrounded by a balustraded terrace. This in turn is supported by a prominent colonnade every fourth spacing of which contains a buttress fronted by a niche. A brick inner cone 18 inches thick helps carry the weight of the lantern to the spring point, while a brick inner dome of equal thickness forms the ceiling and provides "canvas" for the eight monochrome paintings (1715) by Sir James Thornhill. Two stainless steel bands now hold all together.

The interior comprises a well-ordered spaciousness, at times more a majestic accumulation than a unity. But as Wren himself said, "The cathedral is a pile for ornament and for use."

SALVADOR

BAHIA, BRAZIL, LARGELY 18TH CENTURY

THE NORTHEAST COAST of Brazil was the first area of the country colonized by the Portuguese, being closest by sea to their native land. The oldest—and most picturesque—of the Portuguese settlements was Salvador, founded in 1549 and for over two hundred years the capital of Brazil. (Rio de Janeiro, with its more magnificent harbor, became the capital in 1763; in 1960 the capital was moved to the new city of Brasília.)

Guarded by ancient forts and situated on a bluff-like peninsula several hundred feet high, Salvador faces both east and west. Its bay frontage is largely taken by heavy shipping, but the Atlantic waterfront (*opposite*) is alive with colorful coastal lighters. A fine strip of Classic-inspired architecture lends organization and authoritative background to the frenetic activity in front. Note the informal additions behind the main building. The town's upper level, though now largely preempted by the twentieth century, harbors a number of fine colonial buildings, including three notable eighteenth-century churches.

Salvador is one of the few unspoiled waterside cities left in this world: saved by topography.

JANTAR MANTAR

JAIPUR, INDIA, 1726–34

THE STUDY OF mathematics is a highly esteemed pursuit in India—as is astronomy, which has always played an important role in rituals. In fact, the number system that the world uses today is based on Indian-developed, Arab-transported numerals. Reputedly as early as the eighth century, Indian astronomic tables were translated into Arabic, then adopted by the Arabs, and via the Moors taken to Spain.

In Jaipur, the capital of India's northwest state of Rajasthan, we find astronomy's most exotic architectural manifestation in the Jantar Mantar (observatory), built by Maharaja Sawai Jai Singh II in 1726–34. Jai Singh was a legendary soldier, a keen mathematician and town planner, and a passionate astronomer. After laying out the spacious new city of Jaipur, he immediately began the Jantar Mantar near his palace. Smaller editions were later built in Mathura, Delhi, Ujjain, and Benares.

The observatory consists of fourteen major geometric devices for measuring time, predicting eclipses, tracking stars in their orbits, ascertaining the declinations of planets, and determining the celestial altitudes and related ephemerides. Each is a fixed and "focused" tool. The Samrat Jantar, the largest instrument, is 90 feet high, its shadow carefully plotted to tell the time of day. Its face is angled at 27 degrees, the latitude of Jaipur. The Hindu *chhatri* (small domed cupola) on top is used as a platform for announcing eclipses and the arrival of monsoons.

Built of local stone and marble, each instrument carries an astronomical scale, generally marked on the marble inner lining; bronze tablets, all extraordinarily accurate, were also employed. Thoroughly restored in 1901, the Jantar Mantar was declared a national monument in 1948.

An excursion through Jai Singh's Jantar is the singular one of walking through solid geometry and encountering a collective weapons system designed to probe the heavens.

STOURHEAD GARDEN

STOURTON, ENGLAND, 1741–65

THE FORMAL EUROPEAN gardens of the seventeenth and eighteenth centuries, particularly those in France and Italy, were meticulously laid out symmetrical parterres. They created a precise mise-en-scène wherein the observer was spellbound, trapped as it were in magnificence—but still trapped. Versailles is the triumph of such gardens.

The English school of "naturalistic" landscaping, on the other hand, sought to create an informal ambiance whereby all elements of the panorama—woods, trees, lakes, and flowers—were subtly interrelated and deployed, with an architectural accent, preferably a shining Classic temple, providing the focus. Grottoes were often added for witchery. This "landscape gardening," in which the onlooker is a participant in the scene, became enormously popular, with Lancelot "Capability" Brown (1716–83) and Humphry Repton (1752–1818) its most noted practitioners.

Stourhead Garden, an outstanding product of this school, wraps the visitor in bucolic dreams. It was designed by its owner, Henry Hoare II, after he returned from a grand tour of the Continent impressed by Italian gardens and by the misty landscape paintings of Claude Lorrain and Nicolas Poussin. Working with architect Henry Flitcroft (1697–1769), Hoare sought to shape his land into romantic patterns. The informal lake, created by damming the small River Stour, provides the focus, with a Palladio-inspired bridge (*left*) spanning one inlet. Across the water stands the ritual temple, the Pantheon (1753), designed by Flitcroft. Note that the trees are carefully clustered to frame the Pantheon, yet there is a hint of freedom at the left to maintain the depth of landscaping.

Arcadia.

BOM JESUS DE MATOSINHOS

THE BROAD RANGE of hills and mountains that rise behind the east coast of Brazil have been, even in our time, an inhibiting factor for most visitors to this extraordinary land. Yet it was not always thus: when fabulous amounts of gold were discovered in the state of Minas Gerais in 1693, followed by diamonds a few years later, this rude upland region blossomed with a rush of prospectors that lasted until the end of the eighteenth century, when available rewards ran dry.

In the bountiful early days, successful miners put a grateful share of their new wealth into the building of churches, with the result that Minas contains one of the finest—and one of the least visited—collections of colonial architecture to be found anywhere. Reflecting, naturally, the Baroque architecture of the mother country, Portugal, the eighteenth-century churches of Minas Gerais add a notable chapter to world architecture. (Incidentally, Brazil was closer architecturally to Portugal than the widely dispersed Spanish colonies were to Spain.)

One of the most spatially exciting of these churches is Bom Jesus de Matosinhos, which dominates the profile of the hill town of Congonhas do Campo. From the facade—note the richness of the doorway—the church steps down the hillside with a terraced stairway outlined by twelve more-than-life-sized Old Testament prophets. This "tremendous ballet" (George Kubler) of soapstone figures was sculpted between 1800 and 1805 by the Minas-born Antonio Francisco Lisboa (1730–1814), the son of a Portuguese architect and his slave. Lisboa was known as El Aleijadinho, the Little Cripple, because of his deformed hands and wracked body, probably the result of leprosy, which he contracted in his late forties. For much of his long, productive life he had to work with tools strapped to his arms. He was—and is—a too-little-known genius.

MEETING HOUSE

DANVILLE, NEW HAMPSHIRE, 1760

RELIGIOUS ARCHITECTURE has rarely mirrored the faith of its congregations so completely as did the meeting houses of seventeenth-to-eighteenth-century New England. There was no hesitancy, no equivocating, in the creed of the early Puritans, and their black and white, boxlike fanes proclaim this "ostentatious austerity" with bold directness.

Built in 1760 just north of Danville, the meeting house (*opposite*) accommodated both worship and town functions for years, in the dual capacity typical of the day. (Actually town meetings took place long after the congregation had left—until 1878.) Its simple, symmetrical, gabled form is uninterrupted by spire or chimney (the building being heatless), while its upper windows nudge the eaves. Note that the clapboarding is more widely spaced as it rises. Only the Classic framing of the front door eases the starkness—with a touch of help from the random stonework of the foundation.

The interior (*left*) follows the usual meeting house pattern of main door opposite pulpit, box pews—here with airy spindles—and balcony on three sides. Since the Word was central to the religious service, the pulpit and its sounding board are prominent, the pilasters on the side picking up the slight touch of the Classic seen on the front door.

Abandoned at the end of the last century, the Danville meeting house was completely restored in 1936 and is now proudly maintained by the community. Though almost painfully plain, this architectural and social center of village life conveys a fundamental conviction, and a community ethos now long gone.

URNER BODEN
AND THE SWISS
VERNACULAR

SWITZERLAND, TRADITIONAL

IN THE VERY HEART of Switzerland, just over the Klausen Pass from the spot where Uri, Schwyz, and Unterwalden proclaimed their Everlasting League in 1291, stands the tiny hamlet of Urner Boden. With a mere clutch of buildings, at an altitude of 4,555 feet, this might be said to be a microcosm of upland Switzerland: its inhabitants put up with adversity of soil while clustering together under the awesome protection of the northern mountain backdrop.

Swiss vernacular architecture, with its tricultural background and range of building materials, is one of the most fascinating in Europe. When exploring this rewarding country—half the size of South Carolina—one should be sure to take to the hills. The visitor will encounter heavy timber construction in the forested mountains, half-timbering in the region north of Zürich (where advanced construction technique is well known but local wood is only moderately plentiful), and masonry in the Ticino, Italian Switzerland, where stone is almost the only building material.

A fascinating variation of the Swiss vernacular may be seen in the Appenzell region in the northeast (see page 118). Unfortunately many of the mountain hamlets are being deserted today as the young seek a more rewarding life in the industrial valleys.

SAN JOSÉ Y SAN MIGUEL DE AGUAJO MISSION

SAN ANTONIO, TEXAS, 1768–82

FROM ITS FIRST permanent settlement on the North American continent at Saint Augustine, Florida (1565), Spain marched ever westward with its army and priests. Chief among its Texas centers is San Antonio, settled in 1718. Here the first mission of San José y San Miguel de Aguajo was founded in 1720, to be replaced by the second, which dates from 1768 to 1782. As perhaps the most beautiful—and best fortified—of the five Texas missions, San José gives an excellent account of the Spanish contribution to New World architecture, a contribution of originality and sculptural exuberance.

Built of local sandstone and tufa—originally stuccoed and frescoed—and roofed with stone vaults, San José exemplifies the Moorish-Iberian contrast of simple walls playing against richly ornamented doors and windows. Its facade (*right*) is a first-rate example of Spanish Baroque, the elaborateness of the carving surrounding the entry and the window above being outstanding for the church's early date and remoteness. The lovely *ángel* (*opposite*) highlights the cloister, its rectangular pilaster playing with the curvilinear leaves to create a sensitive frame for the child's head.

Suffering grievously through the years, with its roof gone and north wall tumbling, San José was rescued in the 1920s. Its restoration commenced at that time, but was not completed until the 1940s. Architectural historian Hugh Morrison called San José the finest Spanish Colonial facade in the United States.

LE PETIT TRIANON

VERSAILLES IS JUSTLY famous for its enormous palace (1670–82) and the seemingly endless geometry of its gardens. However, for pure delight, its neighbor on the grounds, the Petit Trianon—built one hundred years later—stands alone. It is Europe's most elegant small building. Commissioned for Madame de Pompadour (who died before it was finished), the Petit Trianon was long enjoyed by the court as a retreat from palace formality.

Squarish in plan, approximately 78 feet on a side, it sits serenely at the head of a bowered allée, a tidy block from all directions. A nonmonumental, south-facing courtyard receives the visitor, its rusticated ground floor forming a base for the petit château above. The south and east fronts are of three floors, the west (*opposite*) and north of two, because of grade changes skillfully handled. Three facades of this "small residence" are basically identical: all but the east side project a square central bay framed by four double-height Corinthian pilasters or columns. These embrace three tall windows, properly linteled, with small square windows above. The simple end bays carry identical windows. A well-defined entablature runs across the top, along with a balustrade, to encircle all four sides. The proportions are flawless, beginning with the overall width being twice the height to the roof line.

The west, or private, front gives onto a low terrace beyond which projects a formal parterre lined with clipped elm trees and containing a pool in the middle. (Corinthian columns, not pilasters, are used here for greater visual richness.)

M. Gabriel (1698–1782) served Louis XV throughout much of his long life as Premier Architecte du Roi: he was one of France's most distinguished.

COTSWOLD FARM

GLOUCESTERSHIRE, ENGLAND, TRADITIONAL

THE COTSWOLD AREA of England—west of Oxford, south of Stratford, and north of Bath—forms one of the pastoral highlights of the English countryside. Its architecture, picturesquely at ease in the rolling, sheep-dotted hills, has a unique quality: almost all of the area's buildings are constructed of the oolithic limestone ridge that underlies its wolds (moors). From manors to farmhouses to barns and even stone fences, this material creates a singular homogeneity.

When foundations and basements are excavated, the limestone undercropping, which is not hard when freshly dug, is carefully cut into blocks to form the walls, sliced into thin slates to make roof shingles, and randomly laid up to create fences, which extend the buildings outward so that they embrace the countryside.

In a typical Cotswold farm, such as Ferris Court shown here, there is a tight geometry of all units, bound together by sympathetic angles. Note that the walls are planar statements, including even the dormers, which belong to the wall itself, not the roof. The pitch of the roof is steep, the better to handle the weight of stone shingles.

One material throughout: man and land in symbiotic partnership.

VIERZEHNHEILIGEN

NEAR BAMBERG, WEST GERMANY, 1743–72

A HUNDRED YEARS after Borromini's Quattro Fontane (see page 88), the Late Baroque/Rococo in South Germany and Austria broadened architectural horizons even further. Here will be found architecture, sculpture, and painting vibrant with light and so closely woven together that it is often difficult to know where one art form begins and the other subsides. It is an architecture of joy, and if the cornucopia at times overflows, so be it.

Among the most spritely creations of this short-lived period—the engines of the Industrial Revolution were beginning to herald a new culture—is Vierzehnheiligen, the Church of Fourteen Saints, by Johann Balthasar Neumann (1687–1753). Within its sober, straight-sided outer shell (on preexistent foundations), color and luminosity burst forth. Its inner walls define ovals and circles, its piers vanish into the decorated planes of the ceiling, an altar stands triumphant, while light floods in and color snatches the eye. (As opposed to seventeenth-century Early Baroque churches, daylight plays an essential role.) There is here—as throughout this South German cultural period—a hint of the "confectionery" (Pevsner), but architecture is richer for this hedonism, and so are we.

SAN FRANCISCO DE ASIS

RANCHOS DE TAOS, NEW MEXICO, 1772–1816

IT IS UNDERSTANDABLE why the apse of this mission church (*opposite*) has been so often photographed and painted: it proclaims geometric satisfaction mixed with naive forthrightness. That what we see today is, in a measure, fortuitous does not diminish the impact: San Francisco's tamped-earth buttresses are partially ad hoc additions to sustain walls endangered by floods and erosion. (Similarly, medieval Gothic churches had, on occasion, to call on such subsequent extra buttressing, while Michelangelo's dome atop Saint Peter's has had iron chains inserted at its base to keep it from spreading.)

The Latin Cross main body of San Francisco, measuring 35 feet wide by 125 feet long, is of small interest: the towers are amateurish and the entry out of scale. The interior, with two modest windows in thick masonry walls plus a roof transept, receives only a subdued natural light, in provocative contrast to the clinically illuminated, wood-framed New England meeting houses of the same period. Hot, bright climate versus cool, cloudy—Spanish Catholicism versus New England Congregationalism.

Along with most of the Spanish-founded missions in the Southwest, San Francisco encountered troublesome times when the area's churches were secularized upon Mexico's independence from Spain (1824). General neglect followed through much of the nineteenth century. Happily, restoration and maintenance in this century have been commendable.

THE APPENZELL VERNACULAR
CANTON APPENZELL, SWITZERLAND, TRADITIONAL

THE NORTHEAST CANTON of Appenzell has long considered itself a very special part of the Swiss Confederation. Surrounded by much larger Canton Saint Gall, and divided after the Reformation by religious differences, Appenzell has tended to look inward for its rewards. This self-sufficiency is even today expressed in the colorful Landesgemeinden, in which on the last Sunday in April all eligible men assemble in the open air to elect authorities and pass laws. Their costumes—and those of their families—are among the most colorful and distinctive in Switzerland, and their accent (one gathers) is also special.

Appenzell architecture is unique as well. For several hundred years, Switzerland's noted embroidery has been centered in this area. To provide optimum conditions for work, the houses were designed with continuous strip windows alternating with solid spandrels of standardized wood panels (*opposite*). Modern architecture two hundred years ago! For further cohesion and brightness, all wood is painted a light color (natural wood finish is more usual in Switzerland). With their sharp gables facing south for maximum daylight, with a keenly proportioned wall module, and with cheerful paint enlivening the scene, the buildings create an unusual urban harmony.

In the isolated farm building (*right*), expertise falls off, but basic design and orientation remain. The granary, stable, and house form one attached unit, with the weather wall blank.

NATHANIEL RUSSELL HOUSE

CHARLESTON, SOUTH CAROLINA, 1809

THE MATHEMATICS of the spiral have long tantalized architects and fascinated laymen. In interior domestic spaces, the spiral stair creates a fluid continuity that is doubly emphasized by its rectangular framing. The stair in the Russell House is one of the most graceful to be seen as it whirls, free of wall, to the third floor. The smooth white plaster planes accent its slender mahogany rail, while the stair treads and risers (note their decorative touches) set up a staccato angularity. It is extraordinary technically and esthetically. The architect, alas, is unknown.

As the nineteenth century began, it ushered in both pride and affluence among the generation following the American Revolution; architecture obviously reflected new means. Although the plan of the Russell House shows influences of Britain's Robert Adam (1728–92), such as the ovoid drawing room opposite the stair, the exterior is basically in the then-burgeoning Federal Style. But its greatest distinction is its stair coiling almost through the roof. Long live the helix!

FEDERAL HALL NATIONAL MEMORIAL

NEW YORK, NEW YORK, 1834–42

THE ''DISCOVERY'' of the ruins of Paestum in southern Italy in the 1750s (see page 16), followed by Stuart and Revett's publication in England of *The Antiquities of Athens* (1762), stirred enormous interest in ancient Greek architecture. The Greek Revival period which ensued—first in England and Germany, then in the United States—produced a series of dignified, often stately public buildings. That a reproduction of a two-thousand-year-old temple could properly accommodate nineteenth-century functions was dubious, but American intoxication with Greece and its "stark nobility" remained paramount for some thirty to forty years.

Probably the handsomest, and certainly the most authentic, of these architectural excursions in the Hellenic world is New York's Federal Hall National Memorial (earlier called the Sub-Treasury Building) dominating the fulcrum of Wall Street. Here, amid an armageddon of skyscrapers, march eight Doric columns banded by a sharp entablature and topped by a finely drawn pediment. The whole, alive with sun and shadow, produces one of Manhattan's most animated experiences. The anachronistic yet no-nonsense mathematics of the facade give it self-confident distinction among its fidgety surroundings.

Designed by Town & Davis, who won the commission via a competition, Federal Hall was substantially improved on the interior by John Frazee. The facade, it should be added, is not theoretical but a scaled-down (eleven to twelve) copy of the Parthenon. A plinth of eighteen steps, necessitated by grade fall-off, gives the building some of the dominance of its ancestor on the Acropolis. J. Q. A. Ward's statue of George Washington (1883) counterpoints the architecture. (Washington took the presidential oath of office on this spot in 1789.)

A stage set perhaps, even a straitjacket, but a potent exclamation point at the head of Broad Street.

OAK ALLEY

VACHERIE, LOUISIANA, 1839

FUNCTIONALISM IS NOT usually associated with Greek Revival architecture, but here in the Louisiana delta it is eminently expressed. A great square parasol of a hip roof (four sloping planes), 70 feet on each side, shelters the two-story square house beneath. The roof is upheld by a periphery of twenty-eight Tuscan columns, matching in number the marvelous oak trees in front (the Mississippi River just beyond). The house itself is set back from the columns to create a circumferential double gallery. The galleries are so wide that burning sun and even lashing rains are under control, and the doors and windows can be left open for ventilation. House and columns are of brick (to protect against termites), painted pink as a foil to the fern-draped trees (*Polypodium incanum*). Following the desperate post–Civil War decades, which lasted into this century, the house fell on more than hard times. It was indeed deserted and in danger of collapse until purchased in 1925 and gradually restored by the architect Richard Koch.

The Louisiana plantations are—like the New England meeting houses—very special, unique expressions of American culture.

THE DOME OF THE CAPITOL

THE NATION'S CAPITOL is probably the most instantly recognized building in the United States, in large part for its majestic dome. The design of the Capitol itself reflects the talents of five brilliant architects, the dome only those of the fifth, Thomas Ustick Walter. Construction of this extraordinarily ambitious building—the country was new, untried, and impoverished after the War of Independence—began when George Washington laid the cornerstone on September 18, 1793. It was not completed until December 1, 1863, when Thomas Crawford's statue of *Freedom* was hoisted through the roof and installed.

The history of the bickerings, uncertainties, feuds, and disasters connected with the construction of the Capitol is well known. What is not so generally appreciated is Walter's daring use of cast iron to construct the mighty dome (which replaced an older one). Cast iron was little used in the United States in the mid-nineteenth century; hence its employment here, especially in epoch-making size, was a pioneering achievement. London's electrifying Crystal Palace of 1851, employing cast and wrought iron, also must have been of inspiration to Walter, along with the contemporaneous cast-iron work of James Bogardus for loft buildings in New York City.

The dome Walter designed is visually commanding on the exterior and breathtaking within. Crowning all is a well-turned lantern, surrounded by thirteen columns for the original states and topped with Crawford's bronze statue. The white-painted dome rests on a drum wrapped by a peristyle of thirty-six Corinthian columns, one for each state in the Union at the time of its completion. This robust "banding" and support for the dome delivers much of the sense of scale and orderliness of the overall architecture; it also produces a dome profile that enjoys sun and shadow throughout much of the day. (The domes of Saint Peter's in Rome, see page 72, and Saint Paul's in London, see page 94, both have similar column-lined drums and were obviously influences.) Unfortunately, the detailing of Walter's dome is on the fussy side.

Nesting within the outside dome and forming the ceiling of the Rotunda is a truncated inner dome (*opposite*), with coffered horizontal bands framing its open oculus, beyond which is another partial dome. In 1865, Constantino Brumidi painted a fresco on this inner dome depicting George Washington seated between Liberty and Victory and "surrounded by thirteen maidens in soft-colored robes." The coffered ceiling rests on a cheerful band of thirty-six windows, levitating the dome and admitting beams of sun. Below this runs a continuous painted frieze, begun by Brumidi but finished after his death by others, depicting a cross-section of United States history from Columbus to the Wright brothers.

Thomas Ustick Walter, you served your country admirably: many state capitols bow to your inspiration.

PALM HOUSE, KEW GARDENS

LONDON, 1844–48

THE ANCIENT EGYPTIANS used glass for household vessels and ornaments as early as 1500 B.C., wealthy Romans put it in their windows, the Middle Ages took glass to still-unsurpassed esthetic heights in their cathedrals, Hardwick Hall of 1507 had "more glass than wall," and nineteenth-century industry made glass an inexpensive necessity for all architecture. Glass in the 1800s achieved what might be called its first destiny in the great greenhouses that sprang up in Europe and America, and especially in England. Sir Joseph Paxton (1801–65), who achieved fame with his all-glass, prefabricated—and incomparable—Crystal Palace Exhibition Hall of 1851, was the protagonist of glass in architecture. His conservatory at Chatsworth (1837; now, like the Crystal Palace, destroyed) was one of the great glass pioneers.

Inspired by Chatsworth, and by the eager searching of the times, Decimus Burton and Richard Turner designed the much larger Palm House in London's Royal Botanic Gardens at Kew, where they were the supervising architects. Palm House is 363 feet long by 100 feet wide and rises to a height of 66 feet. Besides educating visitors in the natural world, one of the functions of English greenhouses at the time was to display the exotic range of plants and flowers that flourished in the British Empire.

Ranging from transparent thinness to solid opacity, from plebeian to fantastic in use, glass has been one of architecture's greatest liberators. One of its triumphs can be seen here.

THE WASHINGTON MONUMENT

WASHINGTON, D.C., 1848–85

ROBERT MILLS was the first professionally trained architect born in America—in Charleston, South Carolina, in 1781. Though Mills was known for numerous official buildings (he was long Architect and Engineer for the government), his greatest triumph was in winning the privately organized competition for the Washington Monument (1836). Mills had earlier designed the Washington Monument in Baltimore (1815–25): a Tuscan column resting on a sturdy base and topped by a figure of the president. His proposal for Washington, D.C., was a 600-foot-high squared shaft, barely tapered and almost flat-topped, rising from a huge Greco-Roman peristyle (circular colonnade) wreathed with thirty-two Doric columns plus porch!

The cornerstone was laid in 1848, site problems having caused delays; then, when the monument was some 150 feet high, the Civil War postponed further construction. Mills died in 1855. In 1876, when construction recommenced, George P. Marsh, who was ambassador to Italy, was among those asked for advice concerning completion of the monument. As a student of Egyptian obelisks—there are thirteen in Rome—he immediately suggested that Mills's projected height of 600 feet be reduced to the standard Egyptian proportions of ten times base to height, or 555 feet, a 55-foot width having been established. Marsh also strongly recommended that the circular "temple" base be eliminated and that no decorative trim be used. Finally, he proposed a pyramidal capping of aluminum, a pioneering material for the time.

Finished and dedicated in 1885, the marble-clad pure obelisk, showing a slight change in color, forms a hollow square 555 feet 5 inches high and 55 feet wide at the base and rests on a slab of reinforced concrete 13.5 feet thick. An elevator and 898 steps provide internal communication.

Senmut, the noted Egyptian architect who flourished about 1450 B.C. (see page 12), and who probably commissioned more obelisks than anyone in history, would have applauded this appropriate monument to the Father of His Country. It proudly stands as Washington's happily inescapable attraction, the highest all-masonry tower in the world.

JOHN DOBSON

CENTRAL RAILROAD STATION

NEWCASTLE-ON-TYNE, ENGLAND, 1846–55

METAL — LIKE GLASS —achieved vast new technical heights in the nineteenth century, enabling architects and engineers to span previously unheard of spaces. Iron has Old Testament roots—i.e., "Iron is taken out of the earth" (Job 28:2)—but its early use was basically limited to tools and weapons and remained thus for millennia. Cast iron was perfected towards the end of the 1700s and produced decorative features, then hollow columns and railings. However, being weak in shear and tension, cast iron was of limited use for horizontal beams, rails, and similar demands. It was not until the nineteenth century's perfection of wrought iron and steel—the Iron Age—that strength in tension and shear as well as in compression opened vast new architectural and engineering possibilities. The Bessemer process of 1856 then made steel economically feasible: the railroads were among the first to seize its superior strength, forever changing the world.

Among the boldest early structures that steel made possible were the railroad passenger stations, whose entirely new demands created awe-inspiring spaces.

Filled with steam locomotives breathing fire and spitting sparks, their enormous arched sheds reached unforgettable apogees (Saint Pancras Station in London, for example, has a clear span of 240 feet). Steam engines are now long gone—along with many fine depots destroyed by World War II—but a score or so of the great stations still survive, among them the one shown here.

The Central Railroad Station in Newcastle, a bustling town colonized by the Romans (Hadrian's Wall is nearby), is of unusual interest. Its three lines of trackage curve along an embankment as they swing through the city and station, each group of rails spanned by a separate 60-foot-high arched roof. This top-lit triple sinuosity and the elevated cross-track passerelle give the shed excitement. (Note the steel tie rods of the vaulted roof.) Would that the 600-foot-long facade (not by Dobson) was as fine: design of such unprecedented new dimensions made nineteenth-century architects uneasy!

Incidentally, George Stephenson, the builder of the world's first passenger train (1825), was born nearby.

BANIANE

BANIANE SEEMINGLY HAS been forgotten in the folds of the Aurès Mountains since the Flood and will probably be there, as a cruel statement of life, until doomsday. Molded to every contour of its site in the ravaged landscape of central Algeria, it is at one with nature—and maybe even with God. Its buildings are scrabbled together with local fieldstone, cemented with *pisé* (clay, straw, and pebbles pounded together), and spanned with parts of trees that never saw a blade. Only the chief's house (*upper background*) is stuccoed and whitewashed. In the valley below stretches the oasis that sustains the village.

The region was once a minor Roman outpost, occupied by the Chaouia, a native Berber group, who still cultivate the valleys. May the motionless mother, child, and grandmother in this photograph find peace.

JAMES K. WILSON

PLUM STREET TEMPLE

CINCINNATI, OHIO, 1866

THE THREE-THOUSAND-YEAR history of the design of Jewish houses of worship—like that of most Christian churches—almost always reflected the fashions of current secular architecture. The Roman basilica served as a model for early Roman synagogues—themselves places for assembly as well as for worship—just as it did for early Christian churches.

In the United States, especially during the last century, synagogues and temples were housed in a variety of forms, from semi-Gothic to Islamic to pure Greek Revival (Charleston's Beth Elohim Synagogue, 1840). The Plum Street Synagogue was designed by James K. Wilson, a Cincinnati architect, working closely with Isaac Mayer Wise (1819–1900), the founder of Reform Judaism in the United States. Whereas the Saracenic exterior—complete with two prominent minarets—is competent, the neo-Gothic interior is ablaze with glory. Kaleidoscopic motifs and colors are woven together like a gigantic Oriental rug. Scarce an inch is left unattended—note the stenciling under the arches—but all is carried out with excellent harmony of scale. The bimah (reading platform) is backed by an ark of intricate geometry. The Ten Commandments stand out brightly in the window over the bimah, while the artificial lighting does a commendable job of helping create a joyful setting for worship.

The National Register of Historic Places terms the synagogue a "splendid exotic building": it is this—and a great deal more.

OUARZAZATE AND
THE DADÈS VALLEY

MOROCCO, TRADITIONAL

IN A LANDSCAPE seemingly snatched from the moon, with the snow-capped Atlas Mountains on one side, the Sahara Desert edging the other, and a straggly river seasonally watering the flock, there stretches one of the world's most unusual parades of indigenous buildings. Along this 100-mile-long valley, some 3,000 feet high, caravans from Timbuktu in Mali would periodically wind their way. Until the end of the last century, these caravans, often made up of several thousand camels bearing slaves, gold, and large slabs of salt, would traverse the Dadès en route to the sea and markets. To prevent attack by well-armed merchants and their guards—or perhaps to prey on those less well defended—the native Berber inhabitants along the river erected a series of fortified villages (*ksour*), generally with tribal focus, along with independent family farms. Ouarzazate is one of the most other-worldly of these.

The fantastic architecture of this region, whose closest cousin is South Yemen's Hadramaut, sprang from the ground on which it stands. A low line of stone makes up the foundation, standardized panels of *pisé* form the wall elements, and sun-dried brick is frequently added for decoration. The wall panels are prepared in adjustable wooden frames: for the lower levels the frame produces a panel roughly 3.4 feet thick, a measurement that diminishes for the upper reaches. When a module of pounded *pisé* has hardened, the handy-sized panels are moved up, eventually to eave height. (The rectangular shape and size of the modular formwork of the panels can be seen in the photograph opposite.) Horizontal support for the floors and the roof is of local, and scarce, tree trunks and brushwood. The windowless lower floors are used for storage and stables, the upper levels for living.

Opportunities in the cities of the plain are tempting young Berbers to leave this medieval enclave, and relentless attrition by the elements demands constant upkeep of the buildings. Much has already been lost to fighting and to harsh weather. Morocco—and all of us—would be deprived if this quixotic, almost noble Dadès Valley architecture were to erode away.

GARDEN STEPPING STONES, HEIAN JINGU

KYOTO, JAPAN, LATE 19TH CENTURY

THE JAPANESE ARE ardent worshipers of the land, a characteristic ingrained from youth by looking out of almost any nonurban window. Hemmed by the sea on one side and with a spine of mountains on the other, the islands afford rewarding views in almost any direction. When, on occasion, nature falters, man takes over to produce a series of private gardens; even a tiny plot alongside a humble house reveals affection for the natural world. A suitable single rock, sympathetically framed by appropriate moss, can have religious connotations.

The Heian Jingu (shrine) in Okazaki Park was built only at the end of the last century, but it commemorates the eleven hundredth anniversary of the founding of Kyoto. Its major building is a slightly scaled-down copy of the first Imperial Palace (A.D. 794). The attached garden (*opposite*) forms a welcome retreat from the structured orderliness of the palace architecture, its carefully primitive stepping stones offering a tempting, perhaps daunting, path to the other side. An adventure is made of the mundane, while the eye rejoices in subtle sinuosity.

TRINITY CHURCH

BOSTON, MASSACHUSETTS, 1872–77

BEFORE THE AMERICAN Revolution, only a gradual development had marked architecture in the colonies. In church building, for instance, the famous New England meeting houses underwent a change from an entry on the long side and the pulpit opposite it to the more traditional church plan, but design and material remained basically the same. However, in the years around 1800, a constant parade of changes began, as a fashion-induced and at times puzzling array of "styles" marked each new generation. The Federal Style, neat and tidy, came first, then the formal Greek Revival, the Tuscan, the chameleon Victorian, even a bit of the Egyptian, among others. Then in 1877 an amalgamation of inspirations burst on the scene with Trinity Church in Boston.

Its architect, Henry Hobson Richardson (1838–86), was born in Louisiana and educated at Harvard and the Paris Beaux-Arts. He won the competition for the design of the church and then substantially improved it as the plans developed. Although Richardson once characterized the style of the church as "a free rendering of the French Romanesque," the tower actually recalls Spain, while the refulgent color of the interior suggests the Byzantine.

Whereas Trinity's exterior displays a disparate number of elements, the interior (*opposite*) unfolds a unity of startling richness. In plan a Greek Cross (with four equal arms), the inner space is dominated by the tower which, like a spatial magnet, commands the crossing and carries all with it upward for 103 feet. Every wall, indeed almost every available surface, is enlivened by polychromy, ranging from geometric motifs to realistic portraits of saints and angels, as can be seen in the upper section of the photograph. Stained glass in the windows complements the walls. This colorful embellishment was basically the work of the brilliant artist and stained-glass designer John La Farge (1835–1910), who worked closely with Richardson. Their synthesis of talents produced what many architects feel is the greatest religious interior in America.

Underlying the polychromy one finds a spatial play of arches, half-arches, vaults, cusps, and dramatic wood beams, all coordinated to produce a stunning geometric interplay. The daylight level is low, too low perhaps, but when the skillful artificial illumination comes on, the effect can be magic.

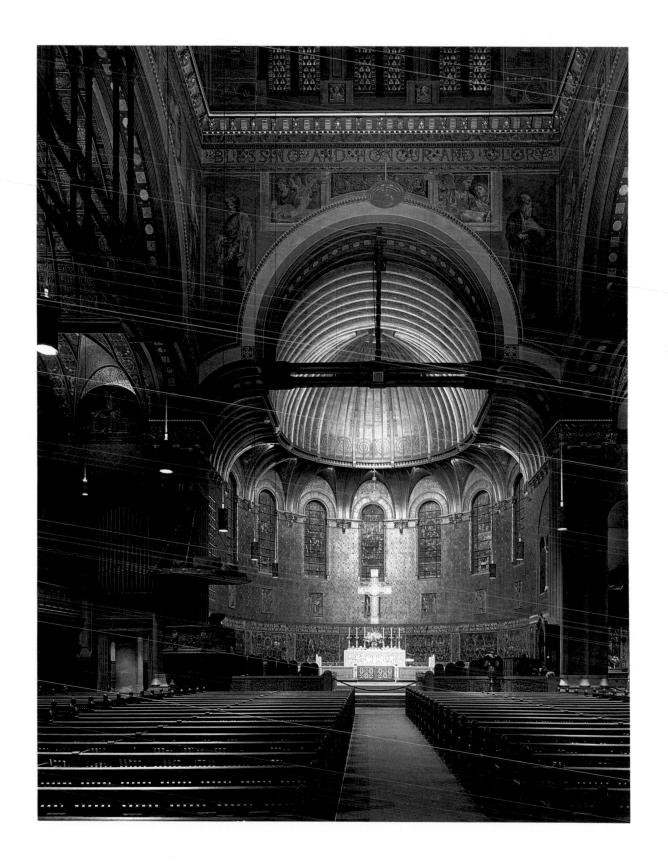

ALLEGHENY COUNTY JAIL

PITTSBURGH, PENNSYLVANIA, 1888

STONE HAS, OF course, been with us since the world began. An early architectural reference is in the Old Testament, Leviticus 14:42, "And they shall take other stones and put them in the place of those [unclean] stones, and he shall take other mortar and plaster the house." It is doubtful, however, that a stone wall has ever been so powerfully fashioned by the hand of man as here in Pittsburgh.

Richardson was one of this country's greatest architects, his powerful, rusticated buildings giving a new (and oft-copied) imprimatur to American architecture. (See also his Trinity Church, page 142.) Here, in his Allegheny County Jail, Richardson diagrammed each stone in a masterful exercise in stonecutting; neither base mold nor cornice weakens the wall's authority as it leaps from the sidewalk. Note that its giant stones gradually diminish in size as they rise— servants, so to speak, of the mighty arch. Voussoirs (the tapered stones of an arch) 8 feet long frame with cyclopean strength an entry to the jail: it is a gateway to hell.

EIFFEL TOWER

PARIS, 1889

GUSTAVE EIFFEL (1832–1923) had produced several intrepid bridges, as well as the iron framework inside the Statue of Liberty, when, following the Franco-Prussian War of 1870–71, he won the competition to create a "heroic structure" for the 1889 Paris Exhibition. The tower he designed reached 985 feet (an even 300 meters), a measure not surpassed until New York City's Chrysler Building of forty years later. When the tower was first projected, its unprecedented height and technical daring caused poets, painters, and philosophers to rail against this "useless and monstrous tower"; when it was completed, most found that *grandeur* had returned to a depressed city.

The head of the Eiffel Tower tempts the sky, while its base sits gracefully at ease on the garden landscape. Built of wrought iron resting on a massive masonry foundation, its four hollow box columns rise gracefully from their corners to coalesce at the top; lattice girders lace all together. The tower's parabolic profile commands respect at a distance; close up, the spatial interaction of the structural members (some fifteen thousand parts) creates constantly changing perspectives. It might be said that what is not there—the structural "voids"—is as important visually as what is—the solids.

One of the supreme achievements of nineteenth-century engineering, the tower combines transparency and kinetic energy to intrigue both artist and visitor.

House and Garden

RIO DE JANEIRO, EARLY 1900S

THOUGH GENESIS 2:8 somewhat ambiguously locates the Garden of Eden "in the east," one branch can be found not far from downtown Rio. Note the discreet garden shelter in the background and the famous Portuguese tiles in the retaining wall. This hillside bower of botanical delight adjoins a private house: from it one enters a world removed from the world. It is called Paradise.

FREDERICK C. ROBIE HOUSE

CHICAGO, ILLINOIS, 1909

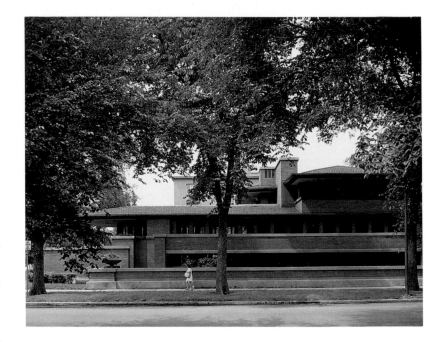

THE ROBIE HOUSE by Frank Lloyd Wright and the Villa Savoye (1929–31) near Paris by Le Corbusier are for many architects the two most significant houses of the twentieth century. Unbelievably, both were scheduled for demolition, and each was saved within only a week of its planned destruction. The greatness of both houses lies in their opening new horizons for domestic architecture and probing the future with unparalleled mastery.

Wright had several ground-hugging Prairie House prototypes to his credit when Frederick Robie asked him to design this suburban house in south Chicago. The Robie possesses its site, reaching out to fuse static house with active sidewalk (*right;* detail *opposite*). There is a calm, even lofty, assurance here little seen in any architecture, particularly domestic, in the early 1900s.

The lower floor contains a billiard room and play space and is set back from the sidewalk by a narrow garden. Above, in one of the serene statements in domestic architecture, stretches the main floor, its 56 feet of continuous French doors capped by a bold cantilever. At the far right end is the built-in garage, among the country's very first.

One of Wright's eternal goals was to open up the house interior, discarding en route the series of box rooms that make up most downstairs. Here the living room and dining room flow together, semidivided by the freestanding fireplace, but tied by the window wall and partaking jointly of the terrace outside. Spatial liberation continues in the two-level ceiling. The second-floor exterior is marked by a short cantilever with a built-in flower box that defines the master bedroom; two other bedrooms adjoin.

With its masterful fingering of site and with its unprecedented flow of inner spaces—the whole wrapped in a conspiracy—the Robie House numbers among the greatest.

EMPIRE STATE BUILDING

NEW YORK, NEW YORK, 1931

STANDING IN LONELY dignity in the midriff of Manhattan, a sentinel by land, a reassuring landmark by air, the Empire State Building is the quadri-faced pharos of the city. And until outstripped by the twin towers of the World Trade Center (1975), its 102 floors were the highest in New York. Though designed at the end of the so-called Art Deco period in the 1920s, when zigzagged appliqués were prominent, its exterior shows little of the frippery characteristic of that "decorated" period. It is, moreover, one of the very few skyscrapers with four facades, not just one facing the avenue.

Zoning required several setbacks, but these were given a skillful buildup of scale at the lower levels, while the tower itself rises unflinchingly. Indented setbacks in the center of each of the long sides help lateral scale. An observation platform and a pylon topped by a television transmission antenna crown all.

Shreve, Lamb and Harmon were the architects of this timeless tower, and H. G. Balcom its brilliant engineer. As Ada Louise Huxtable wrote, "The Empire State Building . . . is a star in its own right, with enduring romantic charisma. Somehow it implies every cherished legend of New York glamor."

Woodland Crematorium

Stockholm, 1940

The so-called International Style of Architecture—the early- to mid-twentieth-century European approach to shelter—did not trickle into Sweden, it arrived with an explosion. The detonator was the famous 1930 Expo (temporary summer fair) in Stockholm, laid out and largely designed by Gunnar Asplund (1885–1940). His works—promptly dubbed "daylight fireworks"—ignited all Scandinavia with their freshness and sparkle. Since that time, little traditional architecture has been built in Denmark, Finland, Iceland, Norway, and Sweden; this northern tier of nations became one of the key proving grounds of twentieth-century architecture, urbanism, and design. Asplund had been noted earlier for his Scandinavian "shaved" classicism, but then architectural winds from the Continent, especially from Le Corbusier, opened his eyes.

The Woodland Crematorium is not only Asplund's finest intertwining of architecture and landscaping, it is one of the spiritual landmarks of the twentieth century. The silent peace of its setting, the detached, poignant cross, and the progressive scale of the complex come together with compelling force. The intimacy between the defined and the infinite, between the man-made and the natural, is not accidental. Asplund carefully had the original hillock built up so that the crematorium and cross would more fully crown the site and so that the trees of the forest beyond would not inhibit the spatial flow through the airy loggia in front of the main chapel. A strategic tree in the garden forecourt of the last of the three small side chapels gives cohesion and accent to the whole. Rising discretely beyond the white marble chapels is the lightly mathematical canopy sheltering the loggia (though without historic reference, there is a hint here of Asplund's classic early period). A statue by Joel Lündqvist rises heavenward through a rectangular opening in the canopy.

"Never before in the 20th century had architecture and landscape been blended so perfectly" (Pevsner).

MARIA KÖNIGIN

COLOGNE-MARIENBURG, WEST GERMANY, 1954

GERMANY HAS HAD a long and distinguished history in twentieth-century religious architecture. However, it was not always easy to persuade clergy and congregations that the church, to be vital, must reflect the culture of the times and build with the forward-looking enthusiasm that had characterized most Christian architecture until the Industrial Revolution. The pioneering churches of the 1920s and 1930s by Otto Bartning, Dominikus Böhm, and Rudolf Schwarz, among others, have borne rewards in the years since the tragedy and destruction of World War II: the postwar churches of Germany are the finest in Europe.

Maria Königin numbers among today's distinguished examples. Its worship room forms a simple, one might say respectful, square 78 feet on a side, its reticence acting as a frame for the glorious window wall (*opposite*). From one end to the other, and from top to bottom, this gray-green *Wunderwald* echoes the world of nature—and the small park outside—with its abstracted trees and cascade of leaves. Designed by the architect and Heinz Bienefeld, it forms one of the great windows of our time. Each of its seven sections, divided by black exposed steel columns, contains two medallions of the Virgin made of small pieces of glass recovered from bombed churches. These not only add color accents but, more important, evoke liturgical symbolism. A clear glass nexus joins the detached baptistry to the nave, and open benches serve for congregational seats. Though not clearly visible here, the ceiling is upheld by four bright vermilion pipe columns, complements to the gray-green glass. Lovely.

MINISTRY OF EDUCATION

RIO DE JANEIRO, 1942

IT IS NOT often that a single skyscraper, especially one merely fifteen stories high and in a then little-visited country, could have a profound influence on architectural thinking around the world. However, Rio's Ministry of Education (now Ministry of Culture) occasioned just such an "enlightenment" when it was finished late in 1942. The essence of its message—one long practiced as fundamental in vernacular building—was control of sun and glare in a hot climate (northern Brazil bestrides the equator). It was the first to use exterior louvers (*brise-soleil*) to keep the sun off glass, a feature that the Swiss-French Le Corbusier had proposed in 1933 for Algiers. Moreover, the office block of the Ministry was elevated 32.5 feet above the sidewalk on freestanding ferroconcrete posts (*pilotis,* another Corbusier suggestion) to create visual airiness and urban freedom. Such an elevated, open ground-level solution was particularly welcome in the narrow streets of downtown Rio.

The building's design was the result of a competition won in 1936 by Lúcio Costa, who then put together a team headed by Oscar Niemeyer. (These two Architects were later basically responsible for the new city of Brasília.) Le Corbusier, who had lectured in Brazil in 1929 and 1936, was asked to be a consultant. His sketches showed both *brise-soleil* and *pilotis,* though his specific proposal for a low-level building, on a different site, was not followed.

The *brise-soleil* that Costa and Niemeyer evolved (*opposite*) consists of movable horizontal blinds, here blue-painted and steel-framed asbestos, whose angles can be manually adjusted to control sun-load on the glass behind. It completely protects the sunny (i.e., north) side, while the shade side is of unscreened glass. As a result of minimum solar heat, the building—in the days before air-conditioning—could be naturally ventilated. Moreover, the varied angles of the louvers give life to the facade. Note, incidentally, that the utility penthouses are sculptural forms, not visual nuisances.

Aside from its pioneering use of *brise-soleil* and *pilotis,* the Ministry of Education also achieves distinction as a brilliant example of early Modern Architecture employed for a governmental building. Most countries in the 1930s and early 40s were still dusting off formalistic Classic Revival for such structures. In addition, several distinguished artists were part of the Ministry's team: Roberto Burle-Marx designed a contemporary roof garden atop the low wing, Candido Portinari decorated the end wall with a tile mural recalling Brazil's Portuguese heritage, and Jacques Lipchitz did the sculpture at the end of the auditorium. Seminal.

NOTRE-DAME-DU-HAUT

RONCHAMP, FRANCE, 1955

UNTIL A FEW centuries ago, the history of the development of Christian church architecture was always forward-looking, its architects (and patrons) seeking to outperform their predecessors. Starting with the Early Christian in 313, when Constantine adopted Christianity, through the Byzantine, the Romanesque, the Gothic, the Renaissance, and the Baroque, each new era pushed the architectural frontiers forward as it reflected the changing culture. Only with the Industrial Revolution did increasingly uncertain man, in an unfamiliar vortex of change, begin to look backward for housing religion; in the process, churches from the past, mostly those from the Gothic Age of Faith, were "adapted" to contemporary needs.

Le Corbusier (1887–1965), considered by many the greatest architect since Michelangelo, inaugurated at Ronchamp a fresh solution for the house of God, one totally of our time yet compellingly religious. Himself a Calvinist, born in Switzerland, but living most of his professional life in France, Le Corbusier confounded, infuriated, and thrilled critics and the public with this Catholic pilgrimage church capping a hill near Belfort. Religious architecture took a glorious step forward with this shrine, with its crazy quilt of windows across the front, outlandish roof, brightly enameled front door, and interior wrapped in curves.

The challenging exterior (*right*) acts as protective armor for the haunting nave, where spaces baffle, no walls are parallel, the ceiling hangs with a perilous sag, the window wall is a chessboard of shapes and colors, and a quiet altar is the focus of it all (*opposite*). The interior measures only 43 feet wide by 82 feet long, but its walls wrap the space with such subtlety that one can be in the church for an hour and not realize that there are three chapels enfolded in their embrace. (The walls' curvature also gives strength to the rubble-stone construction.) Visual "escape" can be found in the slender band of light at the top where the ceiling on the east and south walls rests on small blocks to create spatial detachment from the walls. The incredible hollow-core, concrete-frame south wall varies in width from 12 feet at the bottom to 4.7 feet at the top: its "gallery" of irregularly shaped, painted windows—all by Le Corbusier—are deep set to stimulate circulation toward the altar.

Actually, both outside and in, Notre-Dame-du-Haut demands movement on the part of the observer. As Le Corbusier himself wrote concerning architecture in general, it "must be walked through and traversed. . . . This is so true that architecture can be judged as dead or living by the degree to which the rule of *movement* has been disregarded or brilliantly exploited." Concerning Ronchamp, he said, "In building this chapel I wished to create a place of silence, of prayer, of peace, of spiritual joy."

Louis I. Kahn

SALK INSTITUTE
FOR BIOLOGICAL STUDIES
La Jolla, California, 1966

BIOLOGISTS BELIEVE THAT all life began in the sea; thus, appropriately, the Salk Institute for Biological Studies centers on a pencil-thin channel of water that seemingly runs straight to the nearby Pacific. (Even its travertine paving is laid up to echo this line.) The agora that results (*opposite*) forms one of the noble spaces of twentieth-century architecture.

At one stage Kahn wondered whether the formality of his design was out of keeping with its bucolic setting; whether, for instance, he should put trees in the court. His friend the late Mexican architect Luis Barragán advised him not to put a tree or blade of grass in the space, for it should be "a plaza of stone, not a garden."

Parallel rows of individual offices for the Institute's thirty-six fellows frame the court, their windows angled to face the sea and to present a quiet face to the main approach. From other angles (*right*), the facades create a low-keyed contrast. The detachment induced by this court offers spatial relief, even rejuvenation, to scientists who spend much of their time in the laboratories.

Microscopes and ocean in a curiously haunting combination.

BROOKS HENSLEY CREAGER

ART-DRAMA-MUSIC COMPLEX

PASCO, WASHINGTON, 1971

THE ARID FLATLANDS of eastern Washington state offer little visual pleasure. Notwithstanding an unpromising setting, the architects of this arts complex for Columbia Basin Community College arrived at a solution that is ingenious without and fascinating within.

As a community college, Columbia Basin has many students who have daytime jobs and attend school at night. To create a welcoming, even festive building for this after-dusk student body—and, indeed, for all the community—the architects first created a three-story square block without windows, broken only by a few vertical slits for circulation. On a grass berm surrounding the building, they then placed eight low turrets containing slide and video machines which can project works of art, videos, cartoons, and announcements onto the blank exterior walls!

The inside of this tantalizing box opens onto a labyrinth of unexpected spaces, alive with inner passages and small courts, slashed by ever-changing sunshine and shadow (*opposite*). At night, hidden internal spotlights maintain the excitement. Several overhead passerelles add spatial accents. The building's three levels accommodate art studios, a small theater, music and speech rooms, and administrative offices.

Exterior delight and a magnetic inner focus in an unprepossessing landscape.

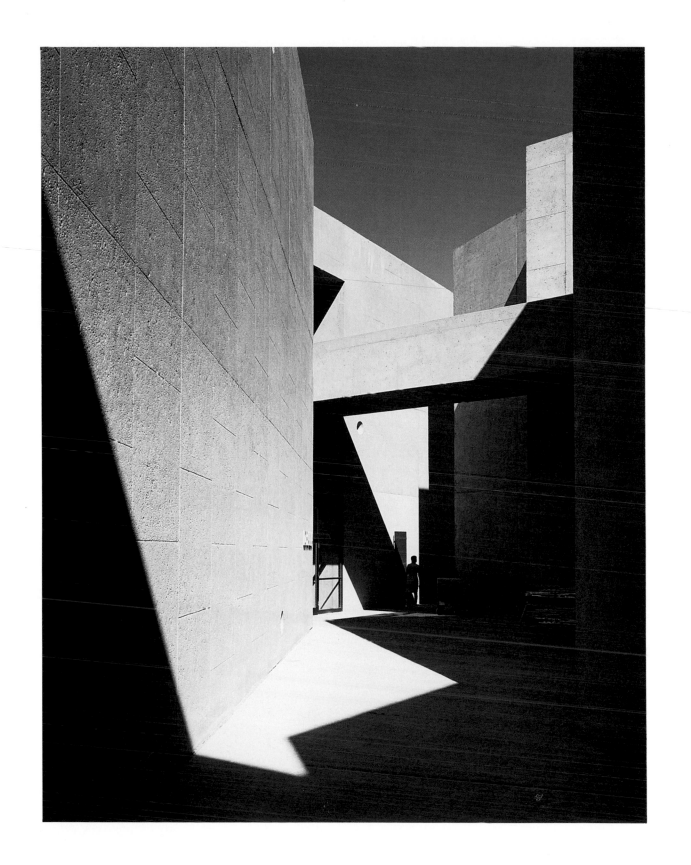

Chase Manhattan Bank and Sculpture

New York, New York, building 1961, sculpture 1972

Urban sculpture through the centuries has enriched many cities, but here it adds an unusual dimension: function. The sixty-story Chase Manhattan Bank building is an unflinching rectangle in New York City's tight financial district. Its exoskeletal slab rises dramatically from the elevated podium on which it sits, its meeting with the horizontal smartly integrated by the open "arcade" of the two lower floors. The major approach to the bank (*opposite*) is from Nassau Street via a few steps to the plaza-like platform. This narrow passageway presented a problem in that visitors would tend, without thinking, to walk right by the main entrance (*far left*) and drop off the end onto William Street. The late Jean Dubuffet solved this dilemma when he installed his *Group of Four Trees*. This 42-foot-high arboreal stop sign nails down the approach as it subtly slows and turns to the left all those heading for the entrance. Moreover, the sculpture brings life to the passage and the podium itself, while its baroque quality counterpoints the mathematics of the architecture. From Pine Street, *Four Trees* acts as a magnet that also marks the entry, while from the lower level of William Street, a glimpse of the sculpture pulls one up the narrow stairs. Built on a steel framework, the "leaves" of the trees are constructed of epoxy-coated fiber glass.

The art of architecture—the function of sculpture.

FOR FURTHER READING

THERE ARE SPECIALIZED books, mostly of a technical nature, on each of the buildings or groups of buildings discussed here. For the general reader—to whom this volume is directed—there are a number of comprehensive histories, which are recommended for broad analyses. Among the probing surveys is Nikolaus Pevsner's *An Outline of European Architecture,* first published as a Pelican paperback in 1943 and reprinted ever since. It provides a provocative, inexpensive overview, but is limited to Europe with a postscript on the United States. Another English classic is Sir Bannister Fletcher's *A History of Architecture,* the nineteenth edition of which appeared in 1987. This inclusive world survey was first published in 1897; the new, vastly updated, 1,621-page volume is crammed with reference data unavailable elsewhere. It is unequaled for research.

Recent general surveys of note are: *Architecture, From Prehistory to Post-Modernism* by Marvin Trachtenberg and Isabelle Hyman (Harry N. Abrams, Inc., 1986), admirable both in text and illustrations; *A History of Architecture* by Spiro Kostof (Oxford University Press, 1985), whose 788 pages imaginatively discuss both buildings and settings; *A History of Western Architecture* by David Watkin (Thames and Hudson, 1986); *Architecture of the Western World,* edited by Michael Raeburn with eight perceptive contributors (Crescent Books, 1980); *The Book of Buildings* by Richard Reid (Van Nostrand Reinhold, 1983), which is not a history but a "topographical guide" with hundreds of small pencil drawings; and *The Architecture of Europe* by Doreen Yarwood (Hastings House, 1974).

An excellent guide-survey of Indian architecture is *The Traveler's Key to Northern India* by Alistair Shearer (Alfred A. Knopf, 1983).

My own three-volume guide, *The Architecture of the United States* (Museum of Modern Art/ Doubleday, 1981), provides comprehensive coverage of notable buildings in America.

ACKNOWLEDGMENTS

THREE LEARNED, lovely ladies helped put this book together, a semantic tidying process that demanded all of their considerable resources. They are: my wife, Dorothea, who shared the delights of many buildings shown and thus meaningfully contributed to my text; Patricia Edwards Clyne, a noted author and historian, who for more than twenty-five years (and three books) has laced up and smoothed out my initial manuscripts with wisdom and perception, then typed them with artistry; and Margaret Donovan of Harry N. Abrams, Inc., who checked facts and figures, then brilliantly reconstructed data and paragraphs. In spite of their efforts, there are, no doubt, errors and dubious conclusions, for which I alone take all blame.

Two long-time friends, both distinguished architectural historians, read much of the text, correcting blunders and naïveté: Prof. James S. Ackerman of Harvard and Dr. Albert Bush-Brown, former chancellor of Long Island University. Their expert help is deeply appreciated. Bob McKee of Abrams designed the book with imagination and flair. Thank you, Bob. Paul Gottlieb, the president and publisher of Abrams and another long-admired friend, audaciously took on this daunting project and carried it to completion with the firm's well-known expertise.

Lastly, a word of gratitude to those foundations whose fellowships through the decades—beginning in 1939—made possible the architectural research and photography shown here.

Bless them all.